HOLLYWOOD IN THE FIFTIES by Gordon Gow

Above: Sophia Loren in *Heller in Pink Tights*

In the same series
produced by THE TANTIVY PRESS
and edited by Peter Cowie:

HOLLYWOOD IN THE FIFTIES

by GORDON GOW

THE INTERNATIONAL FILM GUIDE SERIES
A. S. BARNES & CO., NEW YORK
A. ZWEMMER LIMITED, LONDON

Acknowledgements

STILLS BY COURTESY OF Allied Artists, Cinerama Inc., Columbia, M-G-M, Paramount, RKO, 20th Century-Fox, United Artists, Universal, Warner Bros.

For aid and encouragement, the author wishes to thank Robin Bean, Maryvonne Butcher, Peter Cowie, Raymond Durgnat, Allen Eyles, Joseph L. Mankiewicz, Barrie Pattison, John Sturges, John Webb, Chris Wicking and Cornel Wilde.

Quotations from directors, producers, writers, players and choreographers are from tape-recorded interviews made by the author, and have been broadcast in BBC radio programmes or published in articles for the magazines *films and filming* and *The Dancing Times*.

COVER STILLS
Front: James Dean
Back: Kirk Douglas in *Paths of Glory*

FIRST PUBLISHED 1971
Copyright © 1971 by Gordon Gow
Library of Congress Catalogue Card No. 70-141572
SBN 302 02133 5 (U.K.)
SBN 498 07859 0 (U.S.A.)

Printed in the United States of America

Contents

1. Paradox at Sunset

QUITE EARLY in the Fifties, people said that Hollywood was finished. Twenty years later they said the same thing again. The place was still there, nevertheless; and so was the state of mind which Hollywood engendered and perpetuated, the escapism and the glamour served up as commodities, the inclination to describe an art as an industry. It was during the Fifties that a representative of a major Hollywood studio introduced an actress to me at a London party, with the commendation that she was "one of our most valuable properties." In other words, commerce was predominant. Throughout the Thirties and the Forties it had thrived on regulated efficiency. Hollywood studios worked to proven rules for monetary success. Financiers and audiences knew what to expect. Each big studio had its image, its star personalities, its manufactured dreams, its gilt-edged guarantees against loss on occasional indulgences which might be classified, warily, as art.

This state of mind, this Hollywood, did not finish in the Fifties. It changed. And the change did a power of good. The major cause was financial competition from television. Entertainment and dreams could be had from pictures that moved in the living room. Attendances at cinemas began to decrease alarmingly. Something new was needed; and, in a complacent industrialised art, something fresh had been long overdue.

The change took two forms. On the one hand, a big last stand was mounted to overwhelm the public with demonstrations of the cinema's superiority as a medium, by complex technical devices aligned with subject matter of a primarily simplistic kind. At the other extreme, more interestingly, the outmoded formulae of the big companies began to give place to independent producers, while the companies served as financial backers and as distributors. From this compromise sprang the new spirit of Hollywood, slow to develop but steadily bringing a more individual quality to specific films and delving into areas of sociology which Hollywood had touched upon only with caution in the financial heyday.

Opposite: epitome of bygone glamour—Gloria Swanson in SUNSET BOULEVARD

In retrospect, one can see irony in a memorable film of the year 1950, Billy Wilder's *Sunset Boulevard*. Gloria Swanson, the epitome of bygone glamour, played a fallen star bent upon a comeback and going mad in the quest. A symbol of Hollywood, reluctant to abandon lucrative delusions of grandeur, but not impervious to changing times. In fact, the public needed the change, too: needed to rid itself of persistent delusions. The U.S.A. and the world beyond were not to be lulled or thrilled as easily as in the Thirties, when the Depression could be temporarily forgotten at a musical, and gangsters could be contemplated with awe and envy at a melodrama. In the Fifties, categories began to blur. Where it was valid, in previous books in this series, for writers to proportion their chapters relatively evenly, noting the producers and the masters and the idols and the distinctive studio styles, it would be false to apply such groupings to the Fifties: Hollywood's decade of disruption, of error and trial. Nobody was a consistent master. Even Hitchcock, who came nearest to that status, had his occasional stumbles—the sticky mixture of religion with thrills in *I Confess* (1952) and the uneasy alignment of serious psychology with a very tall tale in *Vertigo* (1958). Yet these two films have their admirers still, and one of the retrospective merits of the decade is its quantity of works that give rise to conflicting opinions, because art thrives on argument and pigeon-holes are dull. Idols, in the Fifties, were no longer merely stars but usually actors. Studios clung to their systems, to be sure, but the stereotyped product was elbowed frequently by the individual thought. *Genres* became more complex: a Western could be a sociological metaphor, a musical could satirise politics and expand into the recognised art form of ballet with a wary but increasing invention, and a thriller more than ever before could dwell upon the motivations of the human psyche.

Hollywood continued to exist, and still does. In the Fifties it often existed away from home. Filming was cheaper in Spain and Italy and Britain; authentic foreign locations were not only more convincing but less expensive than studio mock-ups. Yet the Hollywood look was upon these itinerant works, which is why you will discover films made in New York or London or some other part of the world included among these examples of Hollywood in the Fifties. Often there was confusion on this point, the classic case being *The Bridge on the River Kwai,* hailed as a triumph for British cinema in the U.K. and as a triumph

Hollywood abroad—THE BRIDGE ON THE RIVER KWAI

for American cinema in the U.S.A. The American-financed movie was gradually bringing about an internationalism in film-making, but in the main the style conformed to Hollywood standards of production.

The *Kwai* paradox typified a whole decade of paradox, when Hollywood was at its worst and, equally, at its very best. It was beset by pressures. There was the blight of McCarthyism at the start of the decade, a witch hunt for Communists that ran parallel to the Stalinist witch hunts for "reactionaries" in Eastern Europe. Relationships between the U.S.A. and Soviet Russia had caught Hollywood unawares before, in the Forties when M-G-M completed a light satire on Communism, *Comrade X* with Clark Gable and Hedy Lamarr, just as Russia joined the Allies in the Second World War: hastily, the movie was provided with a written "foreword" to the effect that it was all in fun and not intended as a reflection upon gallant comrades in arms.

When the war ended in 1945, a cold war soon began on account of Russia's domination of countries occupied by Soviet forces in the fight against the Nazis; and, since it was known that the ways of Communism were often subtle, a fear of infiltration in governmental departments of the U.S.A. had led to investigations in which Senator Joseph McCarthy sprang to prominence as a ferocious watchdog, nosing everywhere. Cinema, as the Nazis had proved, was a potent medium for propaganda, and therefore it followed that Hollywood should be examined. But the McCarthy methods were so bulldozing, and the nationwide fear so strong, that many were unfairly victimised. Yet during the Fifties, Hollywood, once devoted to the cosy image of the American way of family life, made numerous films that questioned and doubted the *mores* of society. It was, perhaps, a natural reaction after McCarthy had inadvertently brought himself down by making so bold as to investigate the U.S. Army. Although many people continued to harbour the dread of Communism lurking in their midst, McCarthy himself was widely deplored as a seeker after self-aggrandisement. A tendency to reconsider the social structures and personality traits of American life became prevalent and was reflected, sometimes rather sensationally but often quite sincerely, in Hollywood movies.

This led in turn to other inquiries. The moral influences of cinema upon potential delinquents and criminals, the permissible quantities of violence and sex in movies, were matters of debate; but, of course, this had the effect of drawing people back into the cinemas to see how shocking the pictures really were. The louder the outcry, the more permissive the films became.

Money was to be made from sensation, from anything that seemed a likely prospect. Money obsessed the Hollywood mind. Publicity for movies often informed the public how much the cost had been, as if this information were of vital interest to all, whereas it was really of no consequence to any but the investors concerned. The trait was understandable. Recent changes in the law had prohibited film companies from owning the cinemas in which their own movies were screened. An industry long accustomed to ruling a roost where golden eggs were laid, and to accumulating wealth with practised ease, was suddenly battered in the Fifties by challenges to its security. Among these challenges, the greatest by far was television.

2. A Bigger Screen

To COMPETE WITH TELEVISION, the obvious move was to offer in cinema an experience unavailable in the rival medium. Colour, for a start; but this was not enough, because movies in colour were familiar already and it would not be long before American TV had colour as well. The instant answer was size. Even the largest TV sets gave a far smaller picture than could be viewed in a cinema; so, to accentuate the difference, the cinema screens became much bigger. This was an old idea, used sparingly in the past, when screens had been opened out by hauling away the black borders at the top and sides, and using a magnifier on the projector, to overwhelm audiences with spectacles like the aerial dog-fighting of the First World War in *Wings* (1927), a musical routine in *Whoopee* (1930), a desert battle in *Lives of a Bengal Lancer* (1935) or a volcanic eruption in *Typhoon* (1940). Those old blow-ups on the "magnascopic" screen often sacrificed clarity of definition, but not so badly as in the average enlargement of a snapshot. More detrimentally, the altered shape of the screen for these highlight sequences made nonsense of inserted close-ups of the stars, eliminating foreheads and chins and giving a strange eyebrow-to-lip shot, because directors were not composing their images specifically for the magnascopic treatment which only appeared in certain luxury cinemas. In the early Fifties, a similar blow-up vogue began, hastily and rashly, and it was not confined merely to the spectacular climaxes but was used the whole way through a film designed for normal screens, often with disastrous effects upon composition. In a two-shot, for example, a seated actor might stand up suddenly, and his head would vanish at the top of the frame, leaving the heroine to converse with a decapitated torso. A diligent projectionist, racking away, could adjust the position for a moment or two, but the next cut might confront him with a set-up equally incompatible. Such were the symptoms of panic as exhibitors awaited films made expressly for the widened screen. By tortuous degrees these films came through to them, eventually settling down into CinemaScope or some similar process in much the same elongated shape: the letterbox or pulled-toffee look. Intended to be very big, economy dictated that CinemaScope be adapted to what was termed the aspect-ratio of any given cinema.

Results were so varied that in one vast and expensive cinema in London's West End, the Leicester Square Theatre before its rebuilding, the big screen which had already been installed in haste and used for everything including newsreels and advertisements, all occupying a goodly part of the proscenium space, appeared to shrink for Cinema-Scope, because the black border at the top was lowered and the sides were only slightly extended. This was like peering through the wrong end of a telescope at something intended to impress us by its size. In some parts of the world, CinemaScope arrived before television, exhausting its novelty value before the dreaded competitor had even begun to take its easy advantage.

In the long run, CinemaScope and its near equivalents outpaced the other contenders against television, which included 3-D, Vista-Vision, Cinerama and Todd-AO. At the time, most of the systems claimed to give a three-dimensional illusion, presumably attained by their size and by the concave structure of the screen. But the claim was hardly substantiated. A greater illusion of depth had been received from certain black-and-white movies of earlier vintage, notably *Citizen Kane* (1940), where spatial values depended upon the placement of actors and objects, the dispositions of light and shadow, and deep-focus photography.

First into the fray was Cinerama with a long long colour-travelogue, *This Is Cinerama,* which opened on September 30, 1952, at the Broadway Theatre in New York. Beginning with a formal little sales-talk on an abnormally small screen in black-and-white, it expanded abruptly to engulfing proportions, 23 feet high and 64 feet wide, taking the audience on a vicarious roller-coaster ride. Partial to hovering aerially above canyons and oceans, and to tilting the picture in approximation of the airborne experience, the process induced nausea in some and elation in others. The latter must have been in the majority, because *This Is Cinerama* enjoyed very long runs, as it needed to do: only a limited number of cinemas in populous areas could afford to install the equipment. Photographed by one camera with three lenses, and a reel of film for each lens, the initial Cinerama movies required three projection boxes in a cinema. The central projector threw its beam to the middle of the huge and almost semi-circular screen, while the left-hand box projected to the right, the right-hand box to the left, all in synchronisation (and hard luck if they weren't: I have seen

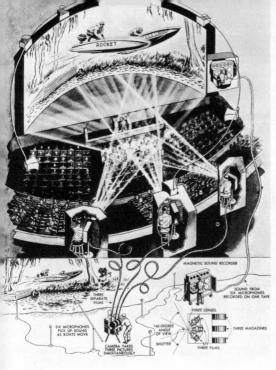

A guide to the triple method of filming and projecting the early Cinerama movies

the worst happen on one eye-searing occasion), creating a composite picture with an arc of 146 degrees. The two "joins" where the images met were frequently obvious to the eye, and apt to shiver; likewise the colour tended to vary slightly on the middle section, and the whole thing worked best when divided firmly by black lines into a triptych effect. All prefigured, of course, by Abel Gance in his *Napoléon* (1927) —save for the sound, which came from numerous speakers for Cinerama, some of them placed behind the screen and others around the auditorium, amplifying the noises and especially the music to such a degree that it would have been a kindness to supply each ticket-buyer

*A somewhat wishful impression of the 3-D impact
—KISS ME, KATE, with Howard Keel, Ann Miller,
Kathryn Grayson*

with a morsel of cotton wool to stuff in his ears. Moreover, from many seats the figures at the edges of the giant frame were distorted, and therefore it took a long time for the process to encompass more than a travelogue, with emphasis on scenery rather than people. Indeed, even when the narration was spoken by Orson Welles for Cinerama's *South Seas Adventure* (1958) there was still a redolence of the old James A. Fitzpatrick "traveltalks" which padded out cinema programmes in the Thirties. The novelty value was considerable, however, for cinemas big enough and wealthy enough to benefit from it.

This left the majority of exhibitors in need of something else. The first possibility was 3-D which held more potential than the anxious film men of the Fifties were prepared to explore. Virtually ignoring the sense of depth, they concentrated upon the illusion of people reaching forth, or objects hurtling out, into the audience. "A lion in your lap" was the advertised appeal of the first 3-D feature, *Bwana Devil* (1952), a thin adventure yarn resembling a Saturday morning serial for younger children, although it did throw in some multi-purpose sex when Robert Stack and Barbara Britton shared their love scene with the audience, each of them leaning forward in separate close-ups to plant a 3-D kiss upon the spectator. As the sense of touch could not be imparted, this seemed like cheating; but one learned to be glad of the deprivation as the 3-Ds proliferated and actors were required to assault their public with all manner of missiles, not excluding a direct spit in the face during *The Charge at Feather River* (1953).

Technically, 3-D was derived from ancient precepts. The photography required two lenses, fairly close together and aimed at slightly different angles to observe the same object, thereby approximating the function of human eyes. If, for example, you sit in a cinema behind somebody whose head seems to obscure part of the screen, let's say the right-hand side, you might find that by closing your right eye the entire screen will be visible, because each eye covers a separate field of vision. 3-D threw its two pictures on the screen together in a system dependent on polarisation, with complementary filters on the projectors. To the naked eyes, the resulting image was an overlapped blur. To compensate, each member of the audience wore Polaroid spectacles. Anyone who wore glasses already, had to cover them with the Polaroids. These had the effect of amalgamating the two pictures into one with a stereoscopic illusion. The cinema had been capable of doing this, without much trouble, from its very inception. Nobody had bothered much about it, especially in Hollywood, apart from a short novelty item or two from M-G-M in the Thirties, known as *Metroscopix* and offering such delights as a senorita rattling castanets in the proximity of the spectator's nose. Somewhat blurry, these old shorts were revived in 1953 by cinemas athirst for any 3-D manifestation available. Overlooked, however, were the superior 3-D shorts exhibited in London at the Telekinema on the South Bank of the Thames during the 1950 Festival of Britain, when abstract and geometrical patterns wafted in space to the accompaniment of music which travelled around the auditorium; there was also a three-dimensional

15

Black Swan *pas de deux,* filmed by Peter Brinson and danced by Beryl Gray and John Field.

Hollywood continued pell-mell with the coconut-shy policy: a case of the U.S. cinema tacitly reverting to its origins as a fairground novelty; and for a time the public rallied. Certain teething troubles were diagnosed, and partially remedied. Definition became better. The wooden cut-out look of the actors, reminiscent of old-time stereoscope photographs, was modulated into a semblance of roundness. And larger screens helped to dissipate the curious sensation of looking through a rectangular hole in a black vault.

The going was frantic. It lasted almost a whole year at high pressure. Quaint tales were told, some possibly true: rumour had it that a certain 3-D frolic was directed by a man of some note who happened to be blind in one eye. But just when the true potential was on the verge of being realised, the bubble burst. Eye-weary critics, who had been impolite to 3-D ever since the Los Angeles *première* of *Bwana Devil* in November of 1952, had grown downright antagonistic by the summer of 1953 and the big studios had begun to hedge their bets. Films made in 3-D became available in "flat" versions for exhibitors who preferred them like that, as many did after the public had received a sufficiency of jolts to the jaw and had made up its corporate mind that 3-D was capable of nothing else. M-G-M's *Kiss Me, Kate* (1953, directed by George Sidney from the Cole Porter stage show, blithely affiliated with *The Taming of the Shrew*) was shown stereoscopically in London at Metro's own cinema, the Empire, where it looked handsome and well-rounded on a big screen, but New York audiences at the Radio City Music Hall were given the flat version. In both forms, as well, came the most fascinating of the 3-Ds, Roy Baker's *Inferno* (1953): the first and only example of the dramatic value of depth, with Robert Ryan isolated in a desert which stretched away towards a distant horizon. This had the very feel of space, heightening our perception of the character's insecurity, and alerting us to the fact that a useful technical advance had been squandered in a short-lived bonanza. By then, no studio cared about 3-D. Neither did some consequential directors, among them Alfred Hitchcock who filmed *Dial M for Murder* three-dimensionally but appeared unperturbed that the majority of his public would have to make do with the flat treatment when it was released in 1954, by which time there was very little 3-D around: "A nine-day wonder," said Hitchcock with his customary blandness, "and I came in on the ninth day."

On the tenth day came CinemaScope. Invented in France in the late Twenties by Henri Chrétien, purchased in the early Fifties by 20th Century-Fox (some things do take time), it was a process similar in effect to Cinerama but on a smaller scale (although much wider than the average screen) and less complicated in photography and projection. The camera's anamorphic lens covered a broad field of vision but virtually squashed the picture to fit the usual 35mm. frames of film. On the developed print, people and objects looked vertically stretched, like reflections in a distorting mirror. For projection, another lens was used to splay the picture out on the expanded screen. Hence its adaptability to screens of various sizes but more or less the same proportions, roughly two-and-a-half times as wide as it was high, and preferably curved but not to such an extreme as Cinerama. In fact it made little difference, except for minimising the danger of distortion at the edges, if there were no curve whatever. Cinerama required a screen constructed of thin strips of tape, louvered to dispel reflections that would otherwise be thrown from one side of the curve to the other. For a long time it was claimed that the CinemaScope curve added a three-dimensional quality, and there are some who still hold to this opinion. The name CinemaScope, incidentally, was supplied by 20th Century-Fox, whose inaugural feature in the process was a popular religious epic from a book by Lloyd C. Douglas, *The Robe,* concerning a Roman who won the robe of Christ in a game of dice before the Crucifixion. The movie turned on a good storm sequence, with the stereophonic sound working directionally to make thunderclaps ring about our heads, and somewhere in the course of it all there was a marvellous backward-travelling view of three white horses racing towards the camera. On the other hand, Richard Burton's hair took on an unwonted purple tinge for the finale, and many of the dialogue passages had the static appearance of a stage production observed by the camera. The general assumption seemed to be that quick cutting on a screen as large as this (ideally at least sixty feet wide and about twenty feet high, or a bit more if possible) would jolt the eye uncomfortably; later, partly because people became used to CinemaScope and partly because screens were not usually so vast, frequency of cutting was resumed. Conversely and quaintly,

many television directors had a feeling that quick cutting was not for them either, because their screen was so small that viewers needed to behold an image for a long time in order to assimilate it; time altered that idea as well.

The Robe had its *première* in the autumn of 1953, a year after the launching of Cinerama; it was directed by Henry Koster; its stars included Jean Simmons and Victor Mature; and it was successful financially. 20th Century-Fox was ready to keep interest alive. The studio released a quantity of CinemaScope films in quick succession, playing safe commercially with screenplays aimed at a fairly low common denominator: adventure stories were to the fore, along with romantic trifles that could incorporate scenic bounty. Jean Negulesco's *Three Coins in the Fountain* (1954) combined eye-filling location shots of Rome with soggy encounters between American girls and Latin males: this was a big hit. At the same time, the CinemaScope process was leased to other major studios, where another spate of hedging bets went on for a time, since nobody could be absolutely certain that a majority of cinemas would convert to CinemaScope after the deflating courtship with 3-D. Caution was the policy at M-G-M again: films in CinemaScope, including *Seven Brides for Seven Brothers* and *Bad Day at Black Rock,* were available in separate versions for exhibitors who did not equip for the new system. But most did, not only in the U.S.A. but eventually throughout the world. Fairly soon, various studios in Hollywood and also in Europe had developed their own anamorphic devices. As director John Sturges put it: "There was a fierce competition between the studios. They didn't tolerate the idea of letting Fox have the dollars by leasing."

Given the panoramic view, however, directors were having trouble in composing pictures for it when the story's requirements concerned the characters rather than the scenery. Sturges was among the first to place human figures effectively in a landscape, forming patterns ideally suited to the CinemaScope proportions, in *Bad Day at Black Rock* (1955). In the same year, Elia Kazan demonstrated in *East of Eden* that the picture within the expanded frame could be tilted, not merely to give the quasi-natural semblance of a 'plane listing over

Opposite: suspenseful solitude and lavish action
for CinemaScope—BAD DAY AT BLACK ROCK (above),
THE ROBE (below)

some diagonal horizon, but to reflect human temperaments as Duvivier had done in the old framing of 1937 for *Un Carnet de bal*. At the other extreme, Otto Preminger had the assurance to keep a character in a medium close shot for minutes at a stretch in *Carmen Jones* (1954), relying upon an expressive face and eloquent song to hold attention, but at the same time placing the character to one side of the frame and concentrating attention in that direction instead of using the familiar dead-centre position for close shots, which only served to emphasise "vacant" space to left and right. Preminger did this twice in an otherwise mobile film.

Bad Day at Black Rock, however, could almost be regarded as a test case for CinemaScope. A confined drama, observing the unities, it had a small cast in a suspenseful plot which unfolded in a few restricted interiors and also outdoors upon the arid earth of a miniscule township and the forbidding countryside surrounding it. Into this weird environment, somewhere in the southwest of the U.S.A., came a thickset stranger with grey hair and only one good arm (Spencer Tracy). He had survived the Second World War, owing his life to a fellow U.S. serviceman of Japanese origin who died and was awarded a medal posthumously. The stranger in Black Rock went to the local hotel and enquired the way to Adobe Flats. He didn't state his purpose, because the reaction to his question was a sullen hostility. In fact he wanted to give the dead soldier's medal to the next of kin, a Japanese farmer. Eventually it was disclosed that several of the Black Rock townsmen had murdered the farmer one bitter wartime day when they were "patriotic drunk." Now, they were making every effort to prevent this enigmatic outsider from unearthing their guilty secret. Sturges disposed his actors in the chairs of the hotel lobby or afoot in the ill-defined streets, in such a way as to use the wide frame geometrically and in doing so to heighten the menacing unity of the people who belonged to the town and to stress the vulnerability of the stranger. From this basic situation, subtleties developed. The killers were strong in their solidarity and yet apprehensive. Grouped inside the hotel, looking out from the window at the bleak landscape which was reflected upon the glass, these men embodied the parched spirit of their town; and then, also reflected in the glass, the stranger was seen, moving across the landscape and also across their line of vision, like a threat: the identification of people and environment, and the intrusion upon their cheerless privacy, were expressed within a single shot in terms both realistic and symbolic. There was also action: the one-armed man drove a jeep towards Adobe Flats, closely followed and repeatedly bumped by a car in which one of his opponents was laughing sadistically, exulting in his vicious two-handed mastery of the steering wheel.

In the main, *Bad Day at Black Rock* made its strongest impressions in stillness, charged with threat—to the individual on the one hand and the group on the other. In 1954, while it was being made, the wisdom of using CinemaScope for such a screenplay was questioned, especially since Tracy had to spend a deal of time alone on the screen as the story approached its climax. Sturges recalls, "At that time Cinema-Scope was considered to be desirable only for thousands of people in huge spectacular productions. I thought it ought to be the other way around. Someone at M-G-M said to me, 'You poor fella, you've got nothing up there but the desert and one man and you're stuck with CinemaScope.' Well, I thought that was about as stupid an observation as could be made—because, if you try to show the isolation of one man in a desert, it's obvious that the more space you have around him the better off you are. I liked CinemaScope and that film certainly gave me a marvellous way to use it. I wish I'd had it a year or so sooner, when I made *Escape from Fort Bravo*: the timing was perfect for it to have been the first Western in CinemaScope. Bob Surtees, who photographed that picture, was as anxious as I was to do it and we could have gotten the lenses but, although some of the M-G-M people were sympathetic to the idea, most of them weren't. There are weaknesses to it, of course: there are times when you just want to see a person's face and the rest is extraneous."

One solution to this lasting problem of the CinemaScope close-up was indicated, also in 1955, in a key sequence of the musical *It's Always Fair Weather,* directed by Gene Kelly and Stanley Donen. As three wartime pals, who meet by arrangement ten years later to compare notes on how civilian life has treated them, Kelly and Dan Dailey and Michael Kidd gave wry evidence that the old rapport of uniformed-conformity had been dissipated to such an extent over the decade that they no longer had anything in common. Dutifully preserving the formalities of their reunion, they sat at a table, ordered drinks and listened to a string ensemble playing "The Blue Danube." In time

Michael Kidd, Dan Dailey and Gene Kelly, ready for individual isolation by the masking process applied to this scene from IT'S ALWAYS FAIR WEATHER

to the music, each man's thoughts were uttered by their disembodied voices: "I shouldn't have come" (pom-pom, pom-pom) . . "This thing is a frost" (pom-pom, pom-pom), and so forth. In each case, the CinemaScope picture of the three of them was masked down, within the frame, to a smaller segment containing just one face, and then another, and then the third, isolated and hemmed in by blackness: each individual excluded by time and experience from what used to be a chummy trio. The masking within frame, as distinct from the manipulation of the screen-surrounds, had its primitive but useful antecedent in oval or triangular masks on the camera lens, employed well before the Twenties in the silent films of D. W. Griffith.

The stereophonic sound that accompanied CinemaScope in many cinemas would relate the disembodied voices in *It's Always Fair Weather* to the exact position on the vast screen where each character was isolated within his separate rectangle, while the masking and expanding was achieved swiftly and smoothly. Stanley Donen was adventurous in his use of the split screen effect as well, giving several different pictures simultaneously in the same frame: he employed this, influentially, in *It's Always Fair Weather* and other movies of the Fifties. But invariably, because the context was light and musical, his example was not followed by makers of dramatic films until the next decade, when multi-imagery heightened the impressions of racing drivers in John Frankenheimer's *Grand Prix* (1966) and masking was applied intelligently for both atmosphere and detail in Richard Fleischer's *The Boston Strangler* (1968). To mask off sections too frequently in the early vogue for CinemaScope would have drawn attention to the disadvantages of the process, although Donen got away with it as a comical diversion.

Other directors began to cast shadows in a crafty way across portions of a room to focus upon an illuminated area of more comfortable proportions. Some just gave up, calling upon their stars to lie down whenever possible to fill the frame, or leaving gaps of unoccupied territory before our eyes. Spectators who were seated very close to the screen grew accustomed to turning their heads to left and right as dialogue was spoken by actors at opposite edges of the frame with a yawning space between them: this viewing from up close eliminated the composition difficulties for some members of the audience who simply couldn't see the screen as a whole. Such was the initial intention, in fact: CinemaScope was planned, hopefully, to fill a very big range of vision from all parts of the cinema, but this only happened in certain luxury houses and by degrees the tendency was to reduce the width of the various scopes when it became obvious that overall composition of every shot was as important as ever, and that long passages without cutting made spectators restive unless a deal of camera movement was employed. The opportunity that was seized by Preminger in those two long phases of immobility in *Carmen Jones* proved to be a rarity: the success, of course, had something to do with Bizet. One really must give Preminger great credit for guessing how strongly the stillness would hold.

He used it for the Flower Song, and later for the Cindy Lou (Michaela) aria, confident that his performers had faces of emotional power, that the updated lyrics by Oscar Hammerstein added piquancy to a familiar storyline, and that the music itself was in these two passages so conducive to stillness that movement would have been an irritant. Simple, yet pretty daring, it did not smack for a moment of photographed theatre, because of the realistic settings, and it contrasted effectively with the profusion of activity in other parts of the film.

Easier for close-ups, and for visual design in general, was Vista-Vision. Trademarked by Paramount, this system's great asset was the combination of size with a more conventional shape. Generally shown in proportions nearer to the old screens, about twice as wide as its height, it could in fact be extremely high and therefore give the impression, when seen at its best, of a CinemaScope screen from which a top border had been hauled up to give more space. Within this frame, pictures were usually devised to allow for the variations of shape that had become a hazard to directors who could never be absolutely certain that what they put inside the frame was going to be seen in its entirety on every cinema screen. Over and above this, VistaVision boasted (and, when viewed under favourable conditions, achieved) a greater clarity of definition than CinemaScope; photographed on film twice as wide as normal, it could also be projected from a print of the same size: 70mm. However, since this involved further expense to exhibitors already tightening belts after their splurges on 3-D and CinemaScope, VistaVision at full strength was only shown to a limited public, while the majority of cinemas made do with a reduction of the 70mm. picture on to the customary 35mm. print, which had intensified definition and no anamorphic squeeze, and could be blown-up to fill big screens by means of an enlarging lens on the projector, still resulting in noticeably greater clarity in colour. Paramount did use it as well for black-and-white movies, among them Robert Mulligan's realistic *Fear Strikes Out* (1957) and Joseph Anthony's stylish interpretation of Thornton Wilder's stage farce *The Matchmaker* (1958). Indeed, movies that ventured warily into a degree of stylisation, or at least heightened the traditional Hollywood concepts of realism, gained most from VistaVision. But usually they were in colour.

One of the first to benefit from the process was Alfred Hitchcock,

*Authentic location, fantasticated plot—Cary Grant
and Grace Kelly at Cannes in TO CATCH A THIEF*

with *To Catch a Thief* (1955) and *The Man Who Knew Too Much*
(1956), both using authentic locations to beguile the eye and at the
same time to point up the lightly fantasticated treatments of plot. *To
Catch a Thief* wallowed satirically amid the wealthy international
drifters of the French Riviera. In prankish form, Hitchcock began
by reviving that useful but forsaken device, the "fade"—in and out.
Rapidly he let us know that a cat burglar was robbing the rich, by
fading in and out of very short fragments: a real cat padding sym-
bolically across rooftops—a woman screaming from a window of
the Carlton Hotel in Cannes, her dementia ironically backgrounded
by the tranquillity of the Croisette in clearest sunlight. Shortly, a
car chase around perilous *corniches* was observed panoramically by
a camera in a helicopter, affording us a heady view of the twisting

mountain road and the sea into which the cars might easily tumble if luck wasn't with them. On sandy *plage,* in placid water, and through a market of radiant flowers, the suspense was counterpointed by the scenery. Mocking the size of the screen, Hitchcock regaled us with a VistaVision close-up of a gently fried egg: in its rich and vulnerable yolk, the hand of Jessie Royce Landis extinguished a lighted cigarette. The shot is doubly typical of Hitchcock, as *cinéaste* and man. It was shorthand symbolism for the nastiness of a rich woman past her prime. In VistaVision it made the spectator's disgust all the greater: few horror shots have drawn from audiences such concerted gasps of revulsion. We must take into account Hitchcock's personal antipathy to eggs in any shape or form. *To Catch a Thief* showed John Williams about to relish a slice of *quiche Lorraine* when Cary Grant forestalled him with the implication that it might be poisoned. Later in the film, haring through a kitchen, Grant himself just breezed through a glass door and closed it, glancing back as an egg aimed in his direction hit the pane of glass and smeared itself nauseatingly across a close shot of his face. On the other hand, cold chicken was positively glamorised in a picnic scene when Grace Kelly offered Grant the choice of breast or leg in a famous *double entendre,* somewhat below Hitchcock par.

The clarity of the comestibles in *To Catch a Thief* was equalled by the VistaVision sharpness applied to objects in *The Man Who Knew Too Much*: the teeth of a dead tiger seized the hand of James Stewart in a frantic-comic scuffle among the products of a taxidermist's craft; the barrel of a gun moved out steadily and blackly from the shelter of a red curtain. It took me four viewings to appreciate this movie, which struck me initially as being rather slow, especially in the early location sequences at Marrakech. Somewhere between my second and third attempts to come to terms with it, I took an opportunity to see the primitive version of the same story which Hitchcock filmed in England in 1934. Imaginative in isolated details, its overall crudity (not least at the climax, when Edna Best's heavily established accuracy with a rifle enabled her to kill the villain without harming her daughter whom he was using as a shield) made the re-make by comparison a paragon of balanced thrills and wit. The major set-piece, an attempted political assassination during a concert in London's Albert Hall, was almost identical in both versions. But in addition to the twenty years of moderation in film acting between the first and second, the melodramatic heightening through VistaVision was exemplified in the distinct range over the vast audience and orchestra and choir, and the close-up detail of the gun protruding from behind the curtain in a box.

Certainly Hitchcock was alert in the mid-Fifties to the dangers of picturesque locations dominating the film. "You don't hold up your story to show a travelogue," he said. "You blend your incidents and play them against the background—you don't separate them from the background. People may complain about the big screens, but films which tend to confine themselves too much are often neglected by the public because they feel they can get the same thing in TV. When a film goes out of doors and into foreign countries, this is something that the public enjoys and which only the movie can give them." This was an opinion that bolstered Hollywood morale and was justified sufficiently when one compared the best of the big screen location shots with actuality material shown on television. Even so, Hitchcock's delight in the technical challenge of confined space had been indulged with great success in 1954 when he restricted James Stewart, as a temporary invalid, to a single room with a *Rear Window* view that limited the range of vision and, thereby, added intense curiosity to the intimations of murder that were glimpsed through the windows and in the gardens of an apartment block across the way. The movie was conformist enough to be in colour, however.

One great hazard for cinema was that colour tended to reveal the contrivance of process work, when actors in a studio were back-grounded by genuine locations photographed separately; in frequent cases, a purple outline hovered disconcertingly around the foreground figures. And, however painstakingly a shot was lit and photographed, the colour quality could be undermined in the printing, as Hitchcock was well aware: "Things can go wrong—the heroine, who might have nice flesh tones, if it's not printed well can come out with a ruddy hue." Conversely, the hero's tan, sun-burgeoned or synthetic, could give place to a deathly pallor in overworked laboratories. The blight continued for years.

Stanley Donen continued his sprightly diversions when he shifted from CinemaScope to VistaVision for *Funny Face* (1956). Not only did he split the screen again to show three people taking different

27

routes around the tourist spots of Paris; he turned the image completely red when Fred Astaire sang the title song to Audrey Hepburn in a photographic darkroom. This was logical enough. "Since it was a movie about fashion photography, the use of colour became very important, almost of primary importance," said Donen. For a sequence in a Left Bank *boîte,* a dance routine was staged in a haze of smoke and misty lights which shone directly into the lens, after the style of the opera sequence in Welles's *Citizen Kane* but in this case for *élan* rather than menace. Yet, in the hidebound and anxious Hollywood of the Fifties, Donen's unorthodox visuals were achieved in the face of "great resistance from technicians and studio officials."

Doc Holliday and the Earp brothers, in the middle distance, arrive for the showdown of GUNFIGHT AT THE OK CORRAL

A muted stylisation was intermittently present in what I consider to be the two best Westerns of the Fifties: *Gunfight at the OK Corral* (1957) and *Last Train from Gun Hill* (1959), both directed by John Sturges who had moved by then from M-G-M to Paramount, where his approach to VistaVision was virtually choreographic. The first of the two concerned the Dodge City marshal Wyatt Earp (Burt Lancaster) and his encounters, which developed into a strong bond of friendship, with the gambler Doc Holliday (Kirk Douglas). The same subject, climaxed by the famous gun battle in Tombstone, Arizona, when Earp and his brothers were joined by Holliday in opposition to the Clanton gang, had been filmed eloquently in John Ford's *My Darling Clementine* (1946). Sturges brought to it a style of his own. Fact probably commingled with legend, as is customary in romantic tales of 19th-century gunmen, but Earp was depicted as a sad man who seemed to regret the violence of his profession, while Holliday's prowess with the gun was underscored by the self-reproach of a well-bred gentleman long since gone to seed. The characters had depth, and the movie had style. Never dwelling upon its visual graces, it was near enough to realism to content a public seeking nothing more than plot, and yet its compositions and patterns of movement had an affinity with painting and ballet. In one succinct fragment, outlaws intruded upon a sedate little dance hall, terrorising the townsfolk: one ruffian leapt to the chandelier, tearing it loose and falling with it to the floor, where it started a conflagration which somebody had the presence of mind to quench with an upturned bowl of punch. In essence this was nothing new, but in execution it was an immaculate evocation of confusion and menace. Again, in a tense period of waiting, Jo Van Fleet as Doc Holliday's woman sat perfectly still in a painterly impression of unspoken anxiety. The resolute walk to the corral for the showdown had a low-angled solemnity, reminiscent of disciplined gladiators approaching an arena where they would prefer not to be. Then, the gunfight itself: a masterly extension of a familiar Western situation; active figures in a landscape, vivid, bullet-ridden, violent, classic.

Last Train from Gun Hill was also dependent upon classic elements, refined and refreshed. Again a rather complex masculine relationship: a series of confrontations between Kirk Douglas as a marshal and Anthony Quinn as a cattle baron whose unruly son (Earl Holliman) had raped and killed the marshal's Indian wife, unaware that the dead woman's husband was his father's old friend. More painterly compositions, indoors and out, as the mature antagonists regretfully faced up to their conflict of intentions: the marshal bent upon revenge for his wife's murder; the wealthy and influential father, angry towards his son and at the same time resolved to keep him alive. Before the climactic shootout at the railroad station, there was prolonged tension while the marshal held the son captive in an hotel room, waiting for the train on which he hoped to take the boy away to stand trial, provided he could run the course from the hotel to the railroad against the gunfire of the cattle baron's henchmen. This entire passage had to withstand some inevitable comparison, especially with *3.10 to Yuma* (Delmer Daves, 1957), a neat if sentimental movie containing a similar plot device in its latter phases and presenting it extremely well.

An unstressed alliance between cinema and ballet was notable again in *Last Train from Gun Hill*. The art of dance and the art of cinema both draw upon a visual language of classic origin. Douglas and Quinn, each representing a different kind of power, were so placed within the frame at given moments to emphasise the shifting ascendancies of their conflict, one man big in the foreground, the other at a distance but still a clear-cut figure. In this film, as in *Gunfight at the OK Corral,* the cinematography of the Hollywood veteran Charles Lang was an important aid to the plastic and spatial concepts of Sturges. The director's own apprenticeship as a film editor was obviously an asset, too, since the character relationships and the placements of actors against various settings were constantly modulated or strengthened by the juxtaposition of set-ups. Sturges maintained one superb set-up, however, in a fairly long take, when Holliman as the son was berated by Quinn, who paced the spacious earth like an actor treading the boards, yet with real ground beneath his feet and the landscape expansive and clear: a subtle equivalent of the more overtly stylised drama attained by Robert Wise and Jerome Robbins in the dance of the Jets at the beginning of *West Side Story* (1961).

Sturges himself described the Quinn-Holliman set-up as "an attempt to relate a scene to the nature of the life the people are leading. I've been around a lot of ranches in the west, and it's a natural thing for people to talk in the open. I felt that the frustration of the Quinn character in that scene was best expressed by him walking around over a great distance and shouting and then turning back on the son, who was just nailed in a corner. Yes, that was choreography, I agree. I'm aware of ballet and of painting, of course, and I enjoy them. They certainly would have affected me, although I've never tried deliberately to imitate them, nor studied them with that thought in mind. But the very awareness of the effects gained by them is bound to be reflected in what I do. Staging is the first function of directing. It's a great weapon. You can put people on the screen in proportion to the importance of the scene. If the relation of the people is right, and if the number of people is right, you can let your eye drift around and accomplish a lot—you don't have to cut back and forth." I asked him to what extent his cutting, in a case like the OK corral gunfight, was pre-planned. He said, "That sort of outdoor location becomes familiar to you as you choose it, and look at it, and study it. You begin to get some kind of pattern in your mind. You also try to have some line of progression so that it will come together, hopefully, at the time you shoot it. Editing is the one other remaining chance. If you shoot enough film, then you have the material with which to change: control the timing, build it up or slow it down. A terribly valuable thing to know about film is that you mustn't try to be so rigid that you commit yourself totally at the time of shooting. Film editing is the *making* of the illusion you're trying to create. The way you put a lot of pieces of film together is the whole story. It's the whole thing."

Less remarkable films in VistaVision were the epic splurges. King Vidor made a brave stab at *War and Peace* (1956), top-heavy beneath its load of Tolstoy mortals from whose muddling profusion Audrey Hepburn emerged delicately as Natasha, while the big screen was handsomely filled with soldiery, as well as a persuasively numbing retreat from Moscow and a most impressive duel at dawn between Henry Fonda and Helmut Dantine, when tension was generated against an ironically serene woodscape covered in snow which glittered in the morning light. On more anticipated lines, the Cecil B. DeMille re-make of *The Ten Commandments* (1956) was histrionic and star-crammed, multitudinous with extras, orgiastic in an old-hat operatic romp around the calf of gold, but technically maladroit in its parting of the Red Sea: this would hardly have convinced an experienced *cinéphile,* even without the new-found clarity which showed up its contrivance derisively.

Unhappily, the VistaVision clarity did not last beyond the Fifties,

*Corn (in the strictly literal sense) was "risin'
clear up to the sky" in the Todd-AO version of
the Rodgers and Hammerstein musical, OKLAHOMA!*

although variants were used for roadshows of big-scale films, a trend
established by Cinerama (eventually ironing out its three-fold jiggles
into a one-camera and one-projector system), and followed up by the
showmanship of producer Michael Todd who had been concerned
profitably in the beginnings of Cinerama but was astute enough to
realise that something of almost equal magnitude could probably be
manufactured without those irritating seams. Therefore he enlisted the

aid of the American Optical Company to devise Todd-AO, to be photographed on 65mm and projected from a 65mm print (or even 70mm) with such powerful light behind it that a cooling system had to be incorporated in the projector. The first movie to use Todd-AO was *Oklahoma!* (1955), from the stage musical by Rogers and Hammerstein with choreography by Agnes de Mille (whose work I have always preferred to that of her Uncle Cecil). Yet again, caution decreed an alternative version, this time in CinemaScope which was the way most of the world saw the completed film. The difference in shape caused Agnes de Mille some worry, in case portions of her dancers would be out of frame, especially the feet at the lower edge of Cinema-Scope when her compositions were designed for Todd-AO which gave more height to the image. She had choreographed the Broadway production of *Oklahoma!,* but this was her first experience of working for cinema and she found that a lot of re-thinking was necessary: "In the theatre, the proscenium arch is a very potent instrument. A girl or boy who runs behind the arch, out of sight, is suddenly out of your life. Anyone stepping out of camera range is virtually still present within a given sequence. A lot of my dances were built on the surprise of people suddenly appearing and leaving—they run across the stage. I couldn't use those things for the film because they didn't make any sense." Her dream sequence was reconstructed in a studio, but the number "Everything's Up To Date in Kansas City" was filmed outdoors (actually in Arizona, because Oklahoma had outgrown the period and too many oil establishments and telegraph lines were in the way): "We could photograph sections of the hills from a high level, so they looked low, like the Oklahoma hills; and the cloud formations were extraordinarily beautiful. I do think a natural setting is a fine thing for certain dances. There is no substitute for sunlight. The fine skies in the desert and the cattle roaming around the screen in *Oklahoma!* give it a lyric quality it didn't have in the theatre. It's a pastoral opera now. It's lost other qualities. It's different. But I find it very beautiful to look at." And so did I, not least in the flight of fancy prompted by the hero's white lie about his purchase of "The Surrey with the Fringe on Top." The director, Fred Zinnemann, trying his hand at a musical with re-markable dexterity, cut away from Gordon MacRae to the visions his song evoked, and in one exhilarating travelling shot the camera moved on the undercarriage of the surrey to give a giantesque power to the

Cantinflas and David Niven, airborne in AROUND THE WORLD IN 80 DAYS

wheels, from which "chicks and ducks and geese" might well run away as the lyrics suggested.

In 1956, Michael Todd's personal extravaganza, *Around the World in 80 Days,* reached a greater number of specially equipped cinemas in the intended form of projection; and, once they were equipped, it was possible for a wider public to catch the Todd-AO version of *Oklahoma!* later on. *Around the World in 80 Days,* lightly based on the Jules Verne novel, pinned its faith on crystal-clear location shots, many of them blissfully aerial, a sufficiency of wit, and a preponderance of stars making cameo appearances around David Niven as the globe-encircling Phileas Fogg and Cantinflas as Passepartout. Michael Anderson, who directed, augmented the location material with episodes filmed on sundry Hollywood back lots: "We were based at RKO, but we used the back lots of 20th Century-Fox, M-G-M, and altogether about five or six studios, where they had acres and acres of permanently built sets—whole streets, cities, railway stations, jungles. Mike Todd hired great sections of them, rebuilt them to his own specifications, and we moved in and shot and then moved out. He wasn't a man to waste money. Every dollar of the seven million the picture cost was on the screen. If he could buy something that was already built, it was obviously more economical." This was refreshing talk at a time when publicity for the big-screen films placed emphasis upon lavish expenditure: anything from ten million to fifteen million dollars was quoted (perhaps truthfully on occasion, for all one knows), the assumption being that people would think a movie had to be good if it cost a lot.

Another Rogers and Hammerstein stage hit was filmed in Todd-AO: *South Pacific,* directed by Joshua Logan who experimented by flooding the screen with dominant colours according to the mood of a song. A purple wash for "Younger Than Springtime," a variety of changing hues upon the face of Juanita Hall as she sang of the Freudian escape-island "Bali Ha'i": the size and the luminosity were perhaps too overpowering, but the idea was interesting, an advance upon the colour tinting used for mood in the silent days (blue for moonlight; red for horrific moments in the 1925 version of *The Phantom of the Opera),* and a prefiguration of the psychedelic lightshows that were to flourish in the latter part of the Sixties.

Right up to the end of the Fifties and beyond, the big-screen variations continued. Several of them were almost indistinguishable from one another, and most of them were made available in modified prints for the less affluent cinemas. As a rule, these humbler versions suffered from a diminishment of clarity. Panavision, a company which was to thrive in the big-screen field during the Sixties, developed another 65mm system known as Camera 65. M-G-M used it for the re-make of *Ben-Hur* (1959). Directed by William Wyler, this was an epic uncommonly well endowed with dialogue: so it should have been, when one considers that, in addition to Karl Tunberg who had the official screenplay credit, the contributing writers included Maxwell Anderson, S. N. Behrman, Christopher Fry and Gore Vidal. Technically, the sharpness

Heston and horses for the BEN-HUR chariot race

of definition proved detrimental to trick effects in a sea battle when Roman galleons fought a Macedonian fleet, and also when Charlton Heston and Jack Hawkins escaped by raft on a sea that looked nowhere near as boundless as intended. But 65mm photography and full-strength projection were the making of the chariot race, a mammoth exercise with trained men and horses belting around a huge arena constructed on the back lot of Cinecitta on the outskirts of Rome. On the screen, it generated such excitement as to distract attention from some rather awkward cutting at points where the charioteers were rounding a bend.

Colour was regarded as *de rigueur* for the big screens, although some directors hankered after the dramatic values of black-and-white. Paramount was lenient and intelligent in this matter, and numerous Vista-Vision movies were filmed to advantage in monochrome. The advantage might often have been on the side of art rather than commerce; but even CinemaScope, announced originally as a process that would always be in colour, was employed sometimes for black-and-white as time went on, and the results were visually quite potent (e.g. Fred Zinnemann's *A Hatful of Rain,* 1957: cinematography by Joe McDonald). Ironically, although Hollywood knew that colour would come to TV, its prevalence in movies of the Fifties was one of the counter-attractions to black-and-white TV, which was the norm in those days, but towards the end of the following decade it became mandatory to film everything in colour with a view to eventual sales of movies to television when their screenings in cinemas had brought in as much money as the public was willing to pay at the box-office. The outcome of this financial necessity was often a compromise in terms of art for both media: television being one thing, and cinema quite another.

3. Words and Images

ORIGINAL SCREENPLAYS, written specifically for cinema, were rare in Hollywood during the Fifties. There had always been a disposition to play safe by adapting material that had been popular already in the form of a novel or a stage play, and amid the growing financial anxiety it was natural for this tendency to become even more prevalent. Yet, in the middle of the decade, almost quirkily it seemed, Hollywood began turning out movies for cinemas which had their origins in teleplays. It was odd, indeed. The assumption that potential film-goers were staying at home watching TV compulsively would scarcely indicate their likelihood to go out and pay money for something they had seen recently by their firesides. One plausible explanation was that certain parties who were making good profits on elaborate movies could offset the concomitant tax problem by losing a bit on these smaller ventures, which belonged to the better of the TV trends, dealing in characters and situations nearer to life than to glamourised escapism, and therefore, in the estimation of many Hollywood minds, they were not reckoned to be hot commercial propositions. The apple cart was overturned by *Marty* (1954, Delbert Mann), a screenplay by Paddy

Chayefsky from his television comedy-drama of the same name, concerning an unprepossessing middle-aged butcher (Ernest Borgnine) and his wary courtship of a woman who considered herself plain and dull (Betsy Blair): a slice of life, credible and touching, spoken in language that caught the essence of everyday speech among simple people. It was launched upon the wider world's critics at the Cannes festival in the spring of 1955, where it took the Grand Prix. It even took the Hollywood Academy Award subsequently, a tribute generally reserved for bigger splurges. Moreover, far from serving any such purpose as creating a beneficial tax-loss, it made money in the cinemas.

As a result, more teleplays were filmed, but the anticipated bonanza did not follow. Several qualified as art, and as trenchant social comment, but as commercial ventures they buttered very few parsnips. *Marty* was produced by one of the independent groups, releasing through United Artists. This set-up had been formed by Harold Hecht, James Hill and Burt Lancaster, and they followed up their unexpected triumph by spending about three times as much money on the filming of another Chayefsky teleplay *The Bachelor Party* (1957), also directed by Delbert Mann, and distinguished by a fine performance from Don Murray as the bridegroom-to-be, doubting but eventually welcoming the ties of matrimony in the course of a dusk-to-dawn stag party, with philosophic aid, *en passant*, from a sad libertine (Carolyn Jones). This was good, but it turned a notably smaller profit. Harold Hecht remarked, "People have come a cropper because they thought they'd have another *Marty,* including ourselves. *Marty* was peculiar to itself."

Low budgets, in Hollywood's corporate estimation, could signify a lowering of status. For a short spate, however, the quality of these superior pickings from TV's profuse crops was influential: promoting awareness of the drama extant in the commonplace, and questioning the validity of accepted social values. Rod Serling's *Patterns* (1955, directed by Fielder Cook: U.K. title, *Patterns of Power*) used strong words to drive home the primitivism of the business world, in which the survival of the fittest animal is depicted in terms of ruthless strategy, and opponents can be demolished by suave manoeuvres that give rise to heart attacks: inhabitants of this urban jungle were brilliantly played by Van Heflin, Ed Begley and Everett Sloane. Reginald Rose's *Twelve*

Opposite: Ernest Borgnine as MARTY

Don Murray (second from right) as the bridegroom-to-be watching a pornographic movie with cronies in the course of THE BACHELOR PARTY

Angry Men (1957, directed by Sidney Lumet) was a dramatic attack upon that established but dubious symbol of democracy, the jury system. Like *Patterns,* it had a subject that the cinema had broached before, but its impact was as strong as its very shrewdly calculated shifts of mind: constricted to a jury room (perhaps too constricted for cinema, disclosing its TV conception too obviously, but compelling in its argument just the same), it presented the fascinating case of a fore-gone conclusion being overthrown by the tenacity and conscience of one juror (Henry Fonda) who, despite persuasive circumstantial evidence, harbours an instinctive doubt about the guilt of a young man whose life depends on the decision these twelve must take. All except Fonda vote "Guilty." Then, by slow and petulant degrees, the majority

Good men and petulant (Henry Fonda seated by right wall)—the jurors are divided at this point in TWELVE ANGRY MEN

are brought around to Fonda's side, until the position is completely reversed and only one clings tenaciously to the initial vote.

All these films were directed by men who had, like the writers, been drawn from television, which Hollywood was beginning to regard, cautiously, as a breeding ground. The recruits seemed eager to stretch themselves in the more flexible medium, although it took a good deal of adjustment. At that period, "live" television was still common in the U.S.A.: cheaper than film, it was deprived of the cinema's margin for error. The tendency was to simplify the visuals. "Both *Marty* and *The Bachelor Party* had been live TV shows, which I like," said Paddy Chayefsky. "I don't like filmed TV because there isn't the time to do really good film on a television programme. But, since they *were* live,

41

the pictures were at best rudimentary, while in the movies of course we had all the mobility we wanted. I don't think we used it properly in *Marty,* but that was our very first movie: the director and I were limited by our own concepts of television techniques. We debated whether to use black-and-white CinemaScope for *The Bachelor Party,* because a large screen might help the feel of the city of New York and Greenwich Village. But colour we didn't want. It's a sombre kind of story."

A decided progression for both Chayefsky as a screenplay writer and Delbert Mann as a movie director was *Middle of the Night* (1959), which had originated as a Chayefsky teleplay and had been converted by him into a stage play, presented on Broadway by Joshua Logan, before the cinema version. In a quietly realistic style, it explored the private agonies of a businessman in his fifties, a widower, finding life

True in every detail of behaviour and thought
—Fredric March in MIDDLE OF THE NIGHT

pretty empty and meaningless until he falls abruptly in love with a girl less than half his age. She works for his clothing firm in a minor capacity, and their liaison gives rise to gossip and reproaches. Without piling on the agony, Chayefsky gave the situation an extra degree of conflict: the girl, divorced from one unsatisfactory man already, is understandably diffident about marrying another who might well prove to be a greater problem in the long run, although the comfort of his love is very important to her. Exceptionally well acted by Fredric March, the man rang true in every detail of behaviour and thought. Kim Novak was tested considerably, and managed very nicely, as the girl. *Middle of the Night* was an incidental sign of Hollywood's more frequent departures into reality at the end of the Fifties. Wryly, an actress well advanced in years had been moved to comment that several leading men of her own vintage were still playing leads, opposite new girls young enough to be their daughters, while she had been cast at the start of the decade as somebody who had to pay a younger man to be her lover. But Chayefsky's insight brought the age-gap pressures into perspective: his ordinary lovers in *Middle of the Night,* human and vulnerable, did not have wealth and authority on their side; voices of derision were not hushed from their ears. They suffered, and one saw that their suffering was unfair. In one memorable image, outdoors on a cold day, March told the girl that he couldn't take any more; his ingrained concepts of propriety, his sense of her uncertainty, brought him low: the weight of his years was palpable. In the end they actually did marry, in spite of every doubt in their minds, and one sensed the rightness of this for each of them. It could not be construed as the normal happy ending, of course; it was a film truthful enough to finish without a full stop, at a point of happiness before a courageous attempt to face the future.

A more poetic view of sexual insecurity was taken in another work that began as a teleplay and then was rewritten for the theatre before it was taken up by Hollywood: *The Rainmaker* (1956) by J. Richard Nash, who scripted all three versions. It explored the indeterminate ground that lies between fact and fantasy. In a Kansas drought, Lizzie Curry (Katharine Hepburn) leads a life parched of love until a hand-to-mouth mountebank (Burt Lancaster) leaps into her family circle with a promise to make the rain pour down if they pay him a hundred dollars. Lizzie, in common with Marty's girl, considers herself plain.

"Somewhere in between" the dream and the reality—Katharine Hepburn in THE RAINMAKER

The conviction has made her aggressive and at first she gives the rainmaker very short shrift, but at night he talks to her of dreams, and brings beauty glowing from her eyes—a feat that always seemed to come to Katharine Hepburn as easily as turning on a light in a darkened room. The conclusion was practical up to a point. The rainmaker, pertinently named Starbuck to emphasise the duality of his nature, told Lizzie of the sustenance to be derived from dreams, which in her opinion was a useless approach to life. She did concede, however, that a feasible existence could be found "somewhere in between" the dream and the reality. She stayed in her small town and married a deputy sheriff, and Starbuck drove away. But it rained as he went, because, within reason, wishes can sometimes be granted. The thing was quite beautifully done, a refinement of sentimentality. It brought to Hollywood the director who had staged it on Broadway, Joseph Anthony, a one-time actor and dancer. He gave the film a moderately stylised air that suited it to perfection, taking note of the barren earth where reality had been eroded to create a blankness from which metaphor could rise. The exteriors around the farmhouse of Lizzie's home circle were quasi-naturalistic, the interiors entirely naturalistic; and yet the bravado of Starbuck, whether in the living room or under the stars, spinning dreams as he and Lizzie sat on bits of agricultural equipment, swept the words into an area of lyricism that was readily accepted because the environment to which it brought relief had been so carefully and cunningly established.

Joseph Anthony had a similar but more testing case, which he tackled with equal if not greater success, in the movie version of Thornton Wilder's *The Matchmaker* (1958), virtually a farce: extremely theatrical. Its pedigree is interesting. Wilder based it on a British play, *A Day Well Spent* by John Oxenford, which was staged in London in the 1830s and revamped as a Viennese romp by Johann Nestroy some years later. Towards the end of the Thirties, Wilder made a new adaptation of it, called *The Merchant of Yonkers*: this (with Jane Cowl in the lead on Broadway, and Max Reinhardt directing) was a failure. But a further doctoring by Wilder, now named *The Matchmaker,* was launched at the Edinburgh Festival of 1954, notable for the breadth and precision and underlying warmth of Ruth Gordon's acting in the central role. This success moved to London for a healthy run, then to Broadway, and on to Hollywood where an extraordinarily fine cast was headed by Shirley Booth. "I don't know why I'm playing it," she said, "because Ruth Gordon was magnificent." But as it turned out, unsurprisingly, Shirley Booth was magnificent too. The matchmaker is a widow, Dolly Levi, given to communing wishfully in solitary moments with the presumably attentive spirit of her late husband. On the practical level, she lays plans to entrap a miserly widower, Horace Vandergelder (Paul Ford), who has piles of money and a general store in the little Connecticut town of Yonkers, *circa* 1880. Dolly wants him, despite his disgruntled ways, as a secure partner for her later years, which are as close as the whiff of poverty that dogs her to try the improbable. Not only matchmaking, but dealing in all manner of petty schemes to raise money, she maintains contact with high life at the Harmonia Gardens Restaurant in New York, where confusion reaches a giddy height of delirium, for herself and Vandergelder and a number of delightful subsidiary characters including a love-starved milliner (Shirley MacLaine) and Vandergelder's two brow-beaten and impecunious store clerks (Anthony Perkins and Robert Morse) who have taken the risk of travelling to the big city for a day and night on the town.

Their journey from Yonkers to New York was briskly represented by a model train crossing an uncompromisingly artificial landscape. Again, Joseph Anthony used stylised elements discreetly, creating a background against which the farcical stuff could be "played up." The humour of *The Matchmaker* has a sentimental core, increasing the director's problem in an intimate medium. The clerks had to hide, for example, in the milliner's shop when Vandergelder turned up unexpectedly: Perkins was confined to a wardrobe where feathery fripperies tickled his nose; Morse scuttled under a low-hanging tablecloth—and these japes were in one sphere while the underlying pathos, muted but important, had to be expressed in the numerous hints of Dolly's anxiety and the emotionally needful quality of the younger characters. Anthony judged to perfection the measure of extravagance that the closer range of cinema would be able to support. He even made it feasible to let the actors, as characters, address the audience in soliloquies and asides. Before the credits at the beginning, Shirley Booth looked right into the lens, scanning "the house" and asking, "Are all you people married?" (Small pause.) "That's nice." Or, again, in the midst of her plot involvements, she could turn to us and say, confidentially, "Life is never quite interesting enough, somehow. You people who come to the movies know that." And Vandergelder, summing up a goodly part of the message, maintained his grouchy demeanour while informing us, like a man in need of group confidence, that "like all you other fools, I'm willing to risk a little security for a certain amount of adventure." All of this was so deft in its blending of hilarity and grace that a musical version of the same subject in the Sixties, *Hello Dolly,* seemed otiose.

Another director to emerge with credit in the Fifties, also with a background in acting, was Richard Quine: a familiar light comedy figure in movies of the Forties, his ability to direct became especially apparent in two more of the borrowings from Broadway, *The Solid Gold Cadillac* (1956) and *Bell, Book and Candle* (1958). Of these, the first needed to be no more than brisked along, sustained by its dialogue and satire (the play was by George S. Kaufman and Howard Teichmann) and given a few easy excursions to the metropolitan outdoors. Judy Holliday crackled as the small investor who began to ask seemingly trivial but increasingly disconcerting questions at a shareholders' meeting, driving the board to distraction and, almost mindlessly, promoting herself to an influential and affluent status. Hardly too sharp as comment upon capitalism, it was a merry study in underdoggery rampant. John Van Druten's play *Bell, Book and Candle* was tricky and yet in some ways more pliant as film material: a drawing room comedy in which leading characters were endowed with supernatural powers to the consternation of an ordinary mortal (James Stewart) whose life was mysteriously changed when an attractive witch (Kim Novak) used her very special influences to gain his love. Her brother, a warlock (masculine for witch), gave Jack Lemmon lively opportunities that he was quick to seize. Other witches were portrayed with relish by Hermione Gingold and Elsa Lanchester. Supernaturally the cinema had advantages over the stage, of course, and there were some useful moody close-ups of a dubious cat named Pyewacket. Quine made much of it all.

As a rule, of course, a play written initially for the stage is visually too confined to be transferred satisfactorily to the free-ranging medium of cinema unless a good deal of adaptation goes on, opening it out. In certain cases, this process might deprive the work of its very essence, and the only viable thing to do is to let well alone, as George Stevens demonstrated to the irritation of some of his admirers in his film of *The Diary of Anne Frank* (1958). Frances Goodrich and Albert Hackett wrote the screenplay which cleaved very closely to their play of the same name, cleverly built up from the diary of a young Jewish girl who, in company with her father and mother and sister and another Jewish family, spent two years in the attic regions above a warehouse in Amsterdam during the Nazi occupation. To convey the trapped feeling, the constant threat of discovery, and the personal frictions of living in such unnatural proximity to one another, a sense of claustrophobia

47

Restricted movement: emphasis placed on details, like this hazard to precious milk in the hideout attic—
THE DIARY OF ANNE FRANK (Millie Perkins, centre)

was imperative. Stevens made so bold as to attempt it in black-and-white CinemaScope, creating the illusion of confinement on a screen designed for impressions of space. The attic, as in the theatre, was divided into several tiny rooms, from which the camera strayed infrequently: notably in a suspenseful episode when the Nazis searched the warehouse and offices beneath them. There were other dramatic advantages: the intrusion below of a thief, and a cat in the attic to be persuaded at all costs not to mew; the shaking of the attic walls as Allied planes dropped bombs on Amsterdam. Yet restriction of movement, going against the nature of the medium, was a constant hazard. Stevens overcame it by taking full advantage of every small detail, every minor sound, and the slow dissolves he employed so beautifully in *A Place in the Sun* were useful again in transitions of time and mood: daringly, almost defiantly, the film lasted nearly three hours.

An easier proposition by far was *Death of a Salesman* (1951, directed by Laslo Benedek). A programme note for the original stage version of Arthur Miller's famous play informed us that the action would take place "in Willy Loman's house—its bedrooms, kitchen, basement, front porch and back yard, and in various offices and places he visits in New York City and Boston." On the stage, all of this was encompassed by a single fixed setting and shrewd lighting effects, designed by Jo Mielziner. Here the past intruded upon the present, as the travelling salesman Loman (Fredric March) contemplated the stages of his decline in a materialistic society and attempted to dissuade his son (Kevin McCarthy) from pursuing a similar course. The progressive technique of the play, according to Elia Kazan who directed it for the stage in New York and London, was an offshoot of Arthur Miller's experience as a radio writer: "He thought of what they call cross-fades in radio drama, and felt they could work in the theatre. I didn't think of them as cinematic, particularly." Yet they were, of course; and the play was ideal for cinema, where Laslo Benedek made beneficial use of the close-up and the possibility of very quiet speech where it was appropriate, as well as merging present and past within a single take. In one classic example of this, Loman was talking with his wife (Mildred Dunnock) in a room of his own house when memory drew him, as it were, towards a door that led to another room—a sleazy hotel room he had shared with a prostitute. Coincidentally, the same kind of cinematic freedom, abolishing the conventional barriers of time and place, was employed that same year in Sweden by Alf Sjöberg for his film of the Strindberg play, *Fröken Julie*. The elementary filmic advantages of being able to cut or dissolve from one place to another (the customary devices of flashback) were eschewed in favour of an even more fluent style, related to theatre, yet given more freedom and expansion by cinema, where the camera leads our eyes in whichever direction is most apt.

A playwright whose theatre pieces were repeatedly adopted by

49

Hollywood in the Fifties was Tennessee Williams. Five of his plays were filmed during the decade: *The Glass Menagerie* (1950, Irving Rapper; summed up neatly by Williams himself: "a very amusing film, and it had the enormous advantage of the participation of Miss Gertrude Lawrence, but unfortunately the poetic quality was not present in the direction"); *A Streetcar Named Desire* (1951, Elia Kazan); *The Rose Tattoo* (1955, Daniel Mann); *Cat on a Hot Tin Roof* (1958, Richard Brooks); and *Suddenly, Last Summer* (1959, Joseph L. Mankiewicz). The transitions from stage to cinema were smooth, possibly because, as Williams put it, "I write my plays in a cinematic style, in many short scenes, longer than 'takes' but much shorter than conventional acts; I've only written one conventional three-act play, *Cat on a Hot Tin Roof*." True as this undoubtedly was, the films were dominated by words: inevitably so, because they were the words of the finest English-language playwright of his generation. Poetic, yet basically real, they heightened character. The words even dominated his original movie script *Baby Doll* (1956, Elia Kazan), written specifically with cinema in mind although it was loosely derived from two short plays from earlier in his career, just as the majority of his theatre plays can be traced back to their origins in his short stories. Indeed, this comparison can make a fascinating study; the material in every case has proved malleable, and the changes of detail and shifts of emphasis illuminate the writer's imaginative and technical prowess.

In terms of character study, the Williams *oeuvre* contains numerous examples of the nomadic male, a prevalent figure in American drama of the period, questing and wandering and bestowing a touch of grace where it is desperately needed, or, in one or two cases, disrupting dreams with the harshness of a realist. One sees the grace more clearly beneath the crude surface of Alvaro in *The Rose Tattoo,* for example, while the brutal streak is most evident in Stanley, the catalyst of *A Streetcar Named Desire*. Comparable figures (though markedly individual ones) are to be found in two major films by other writers. *Shane* (played by Alan Ladd in the George Stevens movie of 1953 from a novel by Jack Schaefer) is the eternal wanderer who happens upon a

Opposite: Katharine Hepburn and Elizabeth Taylor (top) in SUDDENLY, LAST SUMMER, Vivien Leigh (below) in A STREETCAR NAMED DESIRE

Wyoming farmstead at a time of crisis, expiating a guilt of his own by a deed of violence and then going his way, leaving gratitude and dreams in the place he has visited. And William Holden as the nomad of *Picnic* (1955, directed by Joshua Logan and based on a play by William Inge) inflames several women in a small mid-western town through which he passes, stopping to chop some wood and ripple his muscles and carry away, to an uncertain future, a girl (Kim Novak) who would otherwise have withered in the tight-minded community from which he has rescued her. The amalgam of poetry and reality is strong. In the Fifties, a number of writers mixed these salutary potions very well: none better, though, than Tennessee Williams.

For all that, the men in the Williams plays and movies were overshadowed, if only marginally, by women: especially in *Suddenly, Last Summer,* a play in which the leading male character (ostensibly a species of villain, but probably more to be pitied than censured) never appeared, being dead before the curtain rose. And the women in all six of these Williams movies of the Fifties were invariably neurotic, usually romantic, and—even at the dangerously threatening extreme of the possessive mother, Mrs. Venable, in *Suddenly, Last Summer*— creatures for whom Williams had the power to evoke compassion. Williams felt (certainly at that phase of his career, and perhaps continually) that "this is a theme most important to preserve, a truly romantic attitude. Of course, there's also the necessity of having a certain realism and objectivity; but at the same time I think you should base your attitude toward life upon a feeling of idealism or romanticism. I don't see why one can't be physical and spiritual at the same time." More than one actress of note has expressed the opinion that Williams in the Fifties was one of a very few contemporary writers who could provide really effective roles for women. "Maybe," he said, "that's because the women in my family were much more attractive to me than my father. My mother and my sister and my grandmother were great talkers. They expressed themselves very freely and well. My father would express himself mainly in invectives at me. Now that he's dead, I realise that the poor man was most unhappy and felt that his children were somehow alienated from him, and I think he was deeply hurt by this. When I began to write he was pleased, because he thought I would never stop writing poetry. But when I started writing plays, he went to see one—*The Glass Menagerie*—and the house was sold out and they had to put a seat for him in the aisle. He was enormously impressed by that."

One aspect of the Williams plays that must inevitably have attracted Hollywood was their sensation value, their power to shock. In commercial minds, as censorship relaxed, this was a sure bet. But Williams was one of numerous writers using hitherto unmentionable topics to serve the purpose of art and to mirror, or sometimes magnify, life: "I feel that so much of contemporary life is a shocking matter, a really shocking matter. And one is obliged to catch the quality that prevails in contemporary life. If you just read the newspapers in America, you'll see that my plays are far from exaggerations."

The screenplay for *Suddenly, Last Summer* was a collaboration between Williams and Gore Vidal, expanding the long one-acter which had shared a double bill in the theatre with *Something Unspoken* to provide a field night for the actress who played the dominant figures in both: Hortense Alden in New York, Beatrix Lehmann in London. With Katharine Hepburn as Mrs. Venable, the film of *Suddenly, Last Summer* made no concession visually in the long symbolic speech, eloquent and horrific, in which she recounts a journey she made with her late son, Sebastian, "one long-ago summer," to "Herman Melville's . . Encantadas, the Galapagos Islands . . the Enchanted Isles." There, on a beach "the colour of caviar," birds of prey descended from the sky to tear and consume the bodies of newly hatched turtles. Sebastian observed this prolonged massacre for an entire day, under a hot sun. At the end of it he declared that he had seen "God"—and developed a fever. His vision was of a vicious God. It was also a foreshadowing of his own death: Sebastian was eaten alive by a horde of boys who had received money from him for services rendered and grew violent when he refused to give them more. Sebastian was a homosexual of insatiable and ever-questing nature. Sebastian, in fact, was what his mother had made him, a seeker for perfection, laboriously writing one perfect poem each summer in her sublimated view of the situation, but actually searching eternally and hopelessly for the perfect mate, one of his own sex who might sever the umbilical cord with which Mrs. Venable held him captive and estranged him from any other woman but herself.

During the fatal summer of the title, Mrs. Venable was too ill to accompany her son on his usual journeyings, and he had asked his cousin Catherine (Elizabeth Taylor) to go with him instead. The girl discovered, as they travelled, that her purpose was really to act as a decoy, just as Mrs. Venable had always done in her own refined way, to lure young men for Sebastian's delectation. The first of the play's two great speeches, establishing the fatalism of Sebastian, was essentially a surrender to words, magnificently spoken by Katharine Hepburn. The setting of the house where Mrs. Venable lived, in the Garden District of New Orleans, lent a certain appropriate strangeness to the occasion, especially in the exotic garden of tropical plants, retained from the stage version and richly designed by Oliver Messel, augmenting but never overpowering the imagery evoked by the words. In opening out the short play into a film running nearly two hours, excessive advantage was taken of Mrs. Venable's desire that an operation by an experimental doctor (Montgomery Clift) should eradicate the memory of her son's ignominious death from Catherine's mind. Sequences in the asylum to which Catherine had been sent, and from which she was anxious to escape, gave rise to naturalistic little episodes among the hopelessly insane, whose quarters she had penetrated by mistake, reaching out towards Catherine, grasping her ankle, whipping up the sensationalism to a degree inappropriate to "an exercise in making a Grand Guignol story in a literate way": this was the definition of Sam Spiegel, who produced the film, and it was justified by the cinematic interpretation of the second major passage of narrative speech. Here, Catharine's face occupied the right-hand side of the screen while the remainder of the frame was alive with strongly sunlit impressions of Sebastian's horrific summer: his face was never seen, only his legs upon the sand as Catharine was obliged to flaunt herself in a white swimsuit, drawing a crowd of youths to the wire netting that divided the public and private beaches; or Sebastian's back, as his white-suited and vulnerable figure ran desperately from the cannibals who converged upon him eventually, beating tin drums, hacking at flesh, like participants in some pagan ritual. The face of Catharine, throughout all this, did not remain steady in one continuous shot; instead, over to the right, it was subjected to jump-cuts. One was inclined to ponder, unkindly perhaps, on whether it had been found more expedient to shoot the long speech in fragments (Elizabeth Taylor's ability in works of such strength as this would flower in the Sixties, when she acted superbly in films of Edward Albee's *Who's Afraid of Virginia Woolf?* and another Tennes-

see Williams play, *The Milktrain Doesn't Stop Here Any More*—
renamed *Boom* for cinema), but in any case the jump-cutting lent an
extra, if superfluous, touch of neurosis to a passage already highly
charged. Fortunately, the cinematography by Jack Hildyard was in
black-and-white rather than colour, which might have been too much
in the circumstances. This was uncommon, and very intelligent, at a
time when colour was virtually *de rigueur* for a movie of commercial
pretention: art, visual and verbal, had the upper hand.

Primarily, it was verbal. The director, Joseph L. Mankiewicz, accustomed so often to writing screenplays himself, was respectful of other
people's words. A decade later, when the cinema was aglow with
imagery that reflected the restless escape-quest of the psychedelic era,

*A major work in the Hitchcock canon—STRANGERS
ON A TRAIN. Farley Granger as Guy and Robert
Walker as Bruno*

Mankiewicz remarked a bit sadly that his kind of film "demands an audience which is patient with the word. I guess that's out of favour at the moment." It depends, of course, on the quality of the words. *Suddenly, Last Summer* was superior in this respect, whereas numerous films taken from stage plays were ponderously scriptbound. Things were infinitely more visual, as a rule, when a screenplay was adapted from a novel. *Shane* was marvellously spacious, of course: one remembers the pictures more than the words. But even when a novel led on to notable dialogue in a film, the elementary asset of numerous scene changes worked in favour of the visuals. In the ideal examples, word and image might carry equal weight, as they did in Hitchcock's movie of the brilliant Patricia Highsmith novel *Strangers on a Train* (1951). Here there was an intervention of three writers, plus Hitchcock's own inventive brain, between the novel as written and the movie as ultimately screened. One of the writers, incidentally, was no less a thriller scion than Raymond Chandler. Hitchcock and Patricia Highsmith did not meet: they spoke courteously to one another on the telephone. The story was altered somewhat; the novelist was unfazed: "I don't mind at all if they take liberties with my plots because they're trying to do something quite different from a book and I think they have a right to change the story as much as they wish." More appreciated in Europe than in her native U.S.A., Patricia Highsmith is an eminently filmable writer, although she could never write a novel with an eventual sale to the cinema in mind: "It would be like trying to think of a statue when you're painting a picture." The French cinema has seen her potential for the medium more than Hollywood, but *Strangers on a Train* became a major work in the Hitchcock canon, not least because of its basic adherence to the Patricia Highsmith psychology. The "criss-cross" murder scheme proposed by Bruno (Robert Walker) to Guy (Farley Granger) was simultaneously teasing and profound in its implications: "What is a life or two, Guy? Some people are better off dead . . like your wife and my father for instance . . two fellows meet accidentally like you and me. No connection between them at all. Never saw each other before . . . so they swap murders . . . each one has murdered a total stranger. Like you do my murder, I do yours." The words rivet the mind. And, up to a point, Hitchcock lets them, because this encounter on a train will lead to the famous visual set pieces: the intercut tension of Guy's tennis match and Bruno's hand reaching down

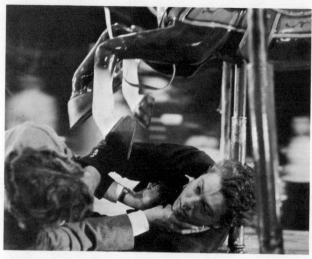

"The band plays on"—Bruno and Guy wrestle beneath the plunging hooves of merry-go-round horses in STRANGERS ON A TRAIN

into a sewer to retrieve a vital cigarette lighter; the strangling across the water from an amusement park, where the distant hurdy-gurdy music of "Strawberry Blonde" accompanies the distorted image of death reflected in the dying girl's spectacles that have fallen to the grass; the lurking of Bruno in the shadows across the street from Guy's home in Washington, waiting with the broken glasses and the happy news that drives Guy almost to the brink of Bruno's own insanity; and the wildly paced repetition of "Strawberry Blonde" conjoined with the whirling of a merry-go-round that has gone beyond control, its inanimate horses bobbing wildly, their hooves plunging towards the wrestling bodies of Bruno and Guy as their world spins round and "the band plays on." From visual imagery—superb black-and-white photography by Robert

Burks—and from dialogue as well, Hitchcock transmuted into purely filmic terms the essence of Patricia Highsmith's concept: the intertangling of the good (Guy) and the bad (Bruno) until one tendency of human nature takes precedence over the other. This is implicit in the novelist's work: "I'm very much concerned with the dualism and the good and evil that exist in everyone to a greater or lesser degree."

This recognition of contradictory strains within a single individual was accepted by Hollywood in the Fifties. It denoted a psychological advance, a gradual overthrowing of the glib distinctions between right and wrong. If we deplored Bruno, we also had a little compassion for him, and a measure of understanding as well. Equally, while we rooted for Guy, we could scarcely overlook his innate smugness, and his sweaty inadequacy when his social-climbing was threatened.

Certainly the demarcation between good and evil had been less distinct than the wishful thinkers would have made it—and did make it still in numerous movies that were popular as palliatives. *Strangers on a Train,* being first and foremost a thriller, merely hinted intelligently at the ambiguities of character, shrewdly pursuing a trend that developed in a rather desultory way in the Forties, when the occasional maverick film would venture beyond the comfortable formula: cases in point were the likable Greenstreet villain of *The Maltese Falcon* (1941, John Huston) and the sympathetic alcoholic played by Ray Milland in *The Lost Weekend* (1945, Billy Wilder). Evil was too easy a word to be applied, without qualification, to the deeds of neurotics. By 1959, partly because controversy was known to be commercial, but also because audiences were being credited with more intelligence, more interest in the complexities of human nature, it was possible to question the ethics of a strict religious order, as Fred Zinnemann did with a nicely judged discretion in his film of Kathryn Hulme's novel *The Nun's Story*. Here was a subject conducive to the process of utilising the cinema's range: it took the heroine, Sister Luke (Audrey Hepburn), to the Belgian Congo, filling the screen with colour and movement that in no way detracted from the central argument. The young girl, tending the sick as part of her determined effort to dedicate her life to God, was repeatedly undermined in this respect by the wry derision of the atheistic surgeon (Peter Finch) with whom she worked. The story afforded Zinnemann a convenient balance of action and dialogue, although it was primarily an intellectual study, all the more interesting because it dealt with one of the most extremely disciplined branches of Roman Catholicism and Zinnemann himself is a Jew. He conceded that this might have been an asset: "One of the Popes once said that Catholics are spiritual Jews, of course. And I found that a great many of the things we were trying to portray touched me very strongly. We all felt that we should remain objective and not favour one side or the other in this case. In certain films you must be deeply involved, but in *The Nun's Story* it was essential for us not to make a comment—to leave the comment to the audience." For all that, the film did raise the questions in no uncertain terms. Its visual strength, in fact, was aligned with its cerebral attitude. The potent images were not those attained on the Congo locations, but the early ones at a convent. The dramatic impact in a colour film of the black and white figures, prone upon the floor in enforced humility, had an austere choreographic quality, reinforcing the feeling of this life which is deliberately "against nature," as the Mother Superior (Edith Evans) pointed out, acknowledging that some, like Sister Luke, could not subdue themselves to its demands. The "good" was to be attained, it seemed, by methods which in other spheres of life would be regarded as "evil"—indeed, sadistic. This being so, it was extraordinary to note the genuine sense of religious dedication which Zinnemann imparted through those characters who were able to adapt themselves to the rigours of their chosen order. He did indeed put both sides of the case, objectively, not without dramatic emotion but never with the slightest trace of sentimentality.

Going against nature, as writers repeatedly remind us, is a human characteristic with varied causes of which the most obvious is the urge to survive. Byron Haskin, a director apt to promote metaphor to good purpose in the context of movies that could easily be pigeon-holed as "adventure" and "entertainment," made a splendid little essay on the eternal primal struggle in *The Naked Jungle* (1953). Taken from Carl Stephenson's *Leiningen versus the Ants,* it concerned an autocrat, wealthy and isolated, ruling a plantation on some distant shore of the Amazon, surrounding himself with luxury in a splendid mansion, marrying by proxy a woman he requires to bring culture as well as sexual solace into his self-centred life. Eleanor Parker had fun (or so it seemed) as the understandably indignant spouse, while Charlton Heston bestrode the property with his customary flair, sweeping all absurdity before him and giving just a hint of pathos to Leiningen's arrogance:

"I don't know how to be second. I can only be first." He was asking for it. Nature gave it to him. Giant ants in military formation, "forty square miles" of them, came inexorably towards his plantation and his houseful of treasures. Human power personified, Leiningen fought. The ants fought back, effortlessly, devouring vegetation on their way, sailing on sturdy leaves across the water of a channel that Leiningen had constructed to forestall them, until at last the wilful human was compelled to burn the priceless furnishings of his mansion, destroying his stronghold to create a wall of fire. The metaphor was strong; and incidentally, of course, the chartered bride saw virtue in her husband at last. While seemingly vengeful nature wrought this transformation upon a martinet, pictures spoke louder than words: the bride's journey up the Amazon, the *objets d'art* in the grandiose dwelling, the forceful physical values of Heston and Eleanor Parker, and the majestic menace of the ants in their multiple seething or in detail-shots of their instinctive wiliness.

By contrast, the animal metaphor in *Track of the Cat* (1954), a panther that symbolised the evil of the world, was never seen. This was a film, from a novel by Walter Van Tilburg Clark, that might very easily have been dominated, indeed swamped, by words—but its director, William Wellman, arranged matters so cleverly that it became a minor masterpiece of visual drama. To appreciate its unique and daring style, one must keep in mind that big screens and colour were in vogue. Wellman used both, yet he minimised their accepted splendours. *Track of the Cat,* visually, was an experimental movie—from a veteran director who was nearly sixty when he made it and who had to his credit such varied films as *Wings* (1927), the original *A Star Is Born* (1937), and *The Oxbow Incident* (1943). In the course of a typical journeyman career in Hollywood, Wellman scaled the heights more than once. *Track of the Cat* was a hard haul. The story was portentous, the dialogue ponderous. Yet the basis was vital. Beulah Bondi played the matriarch of an isolated backwoods family: a mean woman, shielding her cold avarice behind religious *clichés,* imposing such a rigorous morality upon her family that her husband drank himself insensitive all day long, while her eldest son (Robert Mitchum) grew steadily more bitter as he complied with her every wish, assuming a tough masculine veneer, intimidating the younger of his two brothers (Tab Hunter) and trying his hardest to ruin the boy's chances of marriage and escape. Wellman stylised this bigoted environment, grading the

Minor masterpiece of visual drama—TRACK OF THE CAT. Beulah Bondi and Tab Hunter (left of cross) as a victim of the panther is buried

colour down, sometimes approaching monochrome in effect, with much black and white inside the unhappy home and a snow-covered country-side beyond, dotted with pine woods, the trees slender and sharp against the whiteness. Here the panther left his tell-tale footprints, luring humans to the kill: the hunt that would either cost them their lives or remove the evil from their hearts. Mitchum understated the heavy brother quite admirably, shading away from his early bravado and uncouth quips until, in the last stage of the hunt, when the second son was dead and he huddled alone in the cold night beside a meagre fire, running out of matches, reading Yeats ("I sometimes think when I have ceased to be . . . ."), he became the very soul of fear; and the presence of the unseen panther was felt, in the dread he exuded, and the monochromatic stillness of trees and snow.

61

*A life dedicated to the chase—Gregory Peck
as Ahab in MOBY DICK*

The images redeemed the words in *Track of the Cat,* whereas both held equal sway in John Huston's *Moby Dick* (1955). Again a beast of nature to be conquered if possible; and again an experimental use of colour. Huston and his cinematographer Oswald Morris combined monochrome and colour photography, one on top of the other as it were, to suggest old whaling prints: it might not have done this to perfection, but it certainly gave the film a strangeness and often a menacing beauty, apt for the allegorical tale. Huston and Ray Bradbury constructed the screenplay from Herman Melville's classic novel, and Gregory Peck gave a magnificent "thinking" performance, muted and deep-grained, as the vengeful Ahab, dedicating his life to the chase after the giant white whale that had robbed him of a leg. At the Whaleman's Chapel in New Bedford, where the pulpit resembled the bow of a ship, words took command as Orson Welles spoke the famous sermon of Father Mapple. These words were rich in that distinguished voice, rising from a powerful diaphragm to lips that need only breathe the syllables to make them ring: "Jonah, bruised and beaten, his ears like two sea shells multitudinously murmuring of the ocean, Jonah did the Almighty's bidding. . . . Shipmates, woe to him who seeks to pour oil on troubled waters when God has brewed 'em into a gale." And later, Peck, aboard the Pequod, gave bewildered echo: "What nameless, inscrutable, unearthly thing commands me . . making me do what in my own natural heart I dare not dream of doing. . . . Is it I, God, or who—that lifts this arm? . . . And all the time that smiling sky and this unsounded sea—look ye into its deeps and see the everlasting slaughter that goes on." Undoubtedly, a departure from accepted cinema realism was needed to match this language. The colour device, removed from the glossy norm, proved ideal throughout the story, leading helpfully to the extravagant climax in which, in a multiplicity of trick devices, Ahab "boarded" the great whale, which revolved furiously in the sea, entangling him in a harpoon line until he was lashed to the beast, turning with it, striking at its impervious body—"From hell's heart I stab at thee"—while sea spray drenched the camera lens and lingered there in droplets.

Huston began *Moby Dick* with Melville's own device of a first-person narrative spoken by Richard Basehart ("Call me Ishmael"), a disembodied voice belonging to a character who would figure in the story and speak dialogue. For the John Sturges film of Ernest Hemingway's *The Old Man and the Sea* (1958) an unusual narrative speech was employed throughout; here the disembodied voice, speaking in the third person, belonged unmistakably to Spencer Tracy who also appeared on the screen as The Old Man. In fact, there was scarcely any dialogue: an exchange of words between the aged fisherman and the small boy who had faith in his ability to make a big catch. Otherwise the words were culled from the Hemingway novella, in a brilliant screenplay, deceptively simple-seeming but actually quite intricate, by Peter Viertel. John Sturges took over the direction, at the request of the producer Leland Hayward, after Fred Zinnemann resigned from the task. The situation, in the words of Sturges himself, was as follows: "There had been an abortive attempt to make it in Cuba. The things that went wrong there are easily understood. There was a totally realistic approach to the

63

story. Why they took off in this way I don't know. It was a mistake because Spence was obviously not a starving Cuban fisherman." (Hemingway had described the character as "thin and gaunt"—Tracy had grown thick-set over the years.) "Then the Gulf Stream in that area is very rough, and no place to go out with barges and lights and try to photograph somebody in a little boat. And the frustrations of making it were just physical ones. They just worked and worked and worked and got nothing. And Fred quit the film on the premise that it was the wrong way. He simply couldn't accomplish it. I didn't want to touch it. Fred's an old friend—if he couldn't do it, why could I? But Spence and Leland Hayward were friends of mine too, and I really couldn't ignore them because by then they'd decided that it *was* a mistake—this is the reason I did it—and they wanted, for better or worse, to transmit the book as simply as possible. Fred had shot about eight minutes of film, and we used about four of those minutes in the picture. We worked in the Hawaiian Islands, because the water there was practical enough to work in, and we didn't have any problems. We did it as a representation of the book. We put the words against a background that seemed commensurate with them. I wouldn't know how to do it any other way. The words in the book are the thing. We used them simply to hear them: to let Spence say them. It seemed to me that what happened on the screen wasn't as powerful as what was said—literally, the words."

It was something of a breakthrough, if not exactly a trail blazer. Narrative like this was generally restricted to documentary films, a species of cinema that was being largely usurped (and often to good effect) by television. Occasionally the "Call me Ishmael" type of introduction, in first or third person, could establish the necessary details of a filmed novel, or the stream-of-consciousness narration (as in David Lean's *Brief Encounter*) proved useful in heightening characterisation as well as advancing the storyline with an economy that dialogue could not supply. One of the great precepts, too, was Robert Z. Leonard's movie of the Eugene O'Neill play *Strange Interlude* (1932), a triumph of cinema over a theatre original because, on the stage, the actors had to speak their interior thoughts as soliloquies and asides, in addition to dialogue, whereas in the film their lips were motionless in these frequent passages when their disembodied voices were heard on the soundtrack. Certainly *The Old Man and the Sea* would never have lent itself to very much dialogue in any case. The greater part of it left Tracy in isolation, there on the vast sea in his tiny boat, feeling the tug at last, knowing that he was alone no longer but at grips with an antagonist worthy of his respect. The powerful fish, unseen as yet, carried the boat a long distance out to sea, keeping it there for three days and nights. True, the words mattered most. Good words: "He was too simple to wonder when he had attained humility. But he knew he had attained it and he knew it was not disgraceful and it carried no loss of true pride." To those who considered Hemingway insufficiently affirmative, even sentimental, and self-conscious in his use of a simplified structure in prose, the whole thing was anathema. Not so to others, including myself. His choice of words, and his apt differentiations ("A man can be destroyed but not defeated"), encapsulated the will to survive despite a keen awareness of human frailty.

At the same time, the visuals were not minimised by the words. In view of all the technical problems and the process work in which location shots were mated to material shot in a studio, there was the occasional fuzz, the odd and obvious outline that divorced The Old Man's hand from the authentic background of the sea. There was even a flaw in the otherwise brilliant little flashback to a Casablanca tavern where, in younger days, the man had locked hands with a strong opponent and strained with all his might until, after a day and a night of it, the opposing forearm gave way and The Old Man forced it right down to the table: a prefiguration of his triumph over the fish; here, the reverse shots, cutting away from Tracy to the antagonist, showed what looked like some muscular deputy's arm, sitting in for the star, the shirt-sleeve rolled further back from the wrist than Tracy's was in the alternate shots. The scene held, regardless; but if such a glaring continuity error could remain in an expensive production, the pressures must indeed have been considerable. Yet it was a work of visual beauty for most of its length. The director of photography, James Wong Howe, whose quality had always seemed to me most evident in his black-and-white movies, conjured beautiful images of the sea and the sky, of the marlin eventually rising tall from the water, of boats cutting through surf when The Old Man dreamed of youthful days in Africa, and of the gathering of fishermen with furled sails and lanterns to light their way to the harbour in the dark before dawn. The fish, once caught, looked rather unreal, but it was a formidable thing, longer than The Old Man's boat and almost as wide, lashed to the skiff's side for the journey home. Close shots of The Old Man's hands, torn and bleeding after the long battle, bathed and sterilised in the salty sea, were equivalent to the honourable scars of ancient warriors. Given this slightly ambiguous sense of achievement, and the stillness of fulfilment, the film matched the novella's drama as Tracy, very quietly, spoke the astutely placed words: "It was an hour before the first shark hit him." The return to the small village and to the trusting boy, with only the stripped carcass of his catch to prove that trust was justified, held both sorrow and dignity: not tragedy, and certainly not defeat.

4. A Broader Mind

IF McCARTHYISM had the effect of restricting social comment, a glance at the best films made by Hollywood in the Fifties would give one the impression that the whole political uproar had been a storm in a very tiny teacup. McCarthy was not deprived of his office until 1954, and the Korean war called for a surge of patriotism in the first three years of the decade; yet, in 1950, two films directed by Henry King were released, each of them questioning the militant ethos. *The Gunfighter* concerned the plight of a man who wanted to be peaceful but was goaded by a community which relished violence. *Twelve O'Clock High* deplored the inhuman demands of war, and their detrimental effects upon individuals. Certainly, the first of these was a Western and could perhaps be dismissed as a tale of the past, while the second had a certain patriotic element to offset its painful honesty. But neither of them looked as if it had been made in the shadow of political terrorism. Significantly perhaps, both films came from 20th Century-Fox, a studio never loath to prosper on the glossy escapist routes (the more so when CinemaScope arrived), but also highly esteemed for its past excursions into controversial areas. With Darryl F. Zanuck still in charge of production, this policy was carried over from the Forties.

*Tired of running, tired of killing—Gregory Peck
(right) as Jimmy Ringo in THE GUNFIGHTER*

The Gunfighter marked a sharp departure from accepted ideas of the Western as escapism. Although set in the 1880s, it held a metaphor that was pertinent to the mood of the year in which it was first shown. Jimmy Ringo (Gregory Peck) was a professional gunman, notoriously fast on the draw, continually on the run from his enemies, and regarded as the traditional man of action. But he was tired. Tired of running, tired of killing: he wanted no more of it. He was the kind of man with whom numerous members of a 1950 audience could identify: an anti-hero. Despite Korea, despite the fear of Communism, many who had fought in Second World War and had known only five years of peace could identify readily with such a man as Ringo. *The Gunfighter,* equally, was a suspense movie, tense and economic in structure; but it became known as the first of the psychological

67

Westerns, and its impact was deep. Jimmy Ringo returned to the small town of Cayenne after an absence of years, to collect his wife and child and take them to a place where they might begin to live a quiet life. Since the wife had reconciled herself to doing without him, and was reluctant to renew their relationship, Ringo waited for her in a saloon without very much hope, because the sheriff, an old friend and a former gunman himself, had warned him to get out of town as soon as possible. Spatially the film was confined mostly to the saloon. Ringo tried to lie low until his train was due, knowing that he would be challenged to live up to his reputation if he ventured into the streets. But word of his presence spread. Schoolchildren gathered at the saloon window to catch a glimpse of the famous gunman, among them his own son who didn't realise that Ringo was his father. And, naturally, men came into the saloon: a young and brash one, Eddie (Skip Homeier), was determined to prove himself by aggravating Ringo to the point of action. Around Ringo's ears, as he sat by himself in a corner, the terse conversation at the bar rang and riled. "He don't look so tough to me," said Eddie; and an old-timer replied, "If he ain't tough, there's been an awful lot of sudden natural deaths in his vicinity." Ringo's patience wore thin.

In occasional episodes outside the saloon, the social temper of the town was noted. An opportunity for derisive humour was taken at the general store, where women clucked about the dangerous man in their midst, interpolating matter-of-fact orders for sugar and potatoes amid the talk of terror, as if this were just another morsel of gossip to be savoured for what it was worth but hardly to be allowed to interrupt the practical everyday chores. Elsewhere, however, a man was waiting at a window with his gun at the ready, convinced that Ringo had been responsible for the death of his son and eager to take revenge. The eloquent black-and-white photography made its contribution to the tense atmosphere, drawing contrasts between the sunlit street and the comparative gloom of the bar-room, where the composition of shots placed emphasis upon a clock. Time was running out for Ringo.

The clock motif was used to similar effect in Fred Zinnemann's *High Noon* (1952), a movie of even greater contemporary relevance. In that case, the isolated man was a marshal, watching the minutes

*During the Fifties,
Gary Cooper was
among those who
changed the image of
the Western hero*

tick by until a train would arrive bringing to his town a ruthless group against which he must stand alone. His lack of support from towns-people who were too frightened to resist the threat to liberty was seen by many as a direct allusion to McCarthyism—the more so because the screenplay of *High Noon* had been written, brilliantly, by Carl Foreman, one of the men who were obliged to live and work abroad on account of the studio black-listings that resulted from the McCarthy witch hunt. Like certain others, Foreman did well for himself elsewhere and was made welcome again in the U.S.A. after a lapse of time, but initially he was among those whose names could not be attached to screenplays they had written, and who probably counted themselves lucky to be employed at all. This blight didn't hit Foreman until after *High Noon,* which did bear his name and therefore endowed the subject with a heavier political connotation than was intended by its director, at any rate. Zinnemann declared later that he was "primarily interested in showing to what length a man would go to defend his own convictions. It so happened, at the time the film came out, that McCarthy had intimidated large sections of the population, and many people who were innocent were afraid of saying what they thought. So the film seemed to have a bearing, in showing a man who was not afraid of doing or saying what he thought was right. But people reacted to it primarily as drama. The other inference was secondary."

The drama was another suspense exercise, taut and astutely timed, drawing a magnificent performance from Gary Cooper as the marshal; and the tempo was heightened by a trend-setting device, a narrative ballad composed by Dmitri Tiomkin and Ned Washington. Tiomkin was greatly impressed when he saw the rushes, noting Zinnemann's searching close-ups of Cooper in which every pore seemed visible on a face unlike that of the conventional Western hero. The climax was related to tradition, a confrontation in a deserted main street, but the marshal was not the customary hero by a long chalk. His was a true bravery, rooted in fear: if a man is without fear, his deeds require no courage. In this sense the character made a subtle contrast to Ringo in *The Gunfighter,* who was not in the least afraid on his own account, confident in his speed and accuracy on the draw, but who was battling to control his patience and avoid the violence of which he had grown so weary. The same might be said of another Texas gunman played with considerable sincerity by Rock Hudson in a relatively glossy movie, *The Lawless Breed* (1952). Directed by Raoul Walsh and based on the autobiography of John Wesley Hardin, a man hotly pursued by the Texas Rangers in the 1870s, this Western was psychological enough to trace the gunman's origin. He was the child of a hellfire preacher. Hardin claimed that all his killings were done in self-defence, although the Rangers would seem to have doubted this. The film's potentially tear-jerking climax was surprisingly persuasive: Hardin returned from sixteen years in prison to discover that his old gun·was in good working order, carefully preserved by his son, a teenager who had taught himself to twirl the gun with a flourish and was all set to follow in his father's glamorous footsteps. At this point, with old-fashioned fervour, the image whirled into a flashback montage of the many gunfights the father had experienced, after which Rock Hudson dealt the boy a savage blow. In the context, so dangerously close to corn, the moment was electrifying. The timeworn let-out of putting a crime-does-not-pay

*Displacing old notions of heroism—Gregory Peck
(seated) as the general in TWELVE O'CLOCK HIGH;
James Mason as the spy in FIVE FINGERS*

tag on the last reel of a violent spree was not enough by 1952 in
any movie that had the slightest respect for itself. *The Lawless Breed*
was sentimental, but it was also tough in the right places.

The other Henry King film of 1950, *Twelve O'Clock High,* had
a sharper sting than the Westerns. It denoted a progression in war
films, similar to that which had been evident after the First World
War. Propaganda for the services, *de rigueur* while the war was going
on, would be sustained to no small extent on account of Korea and
the cold war against Communism. But, cheek by jowl with all that,
the anti-war film emerged again. *Twelve O'Clock High* was the spear-
head: here was a counter-attack, a militant bid for peace in which
notions of heroism gave place, warily and still a bit sentimentally, to

the contention that war is an uncivilised activity. This film concerned the "maximum effort" demanded of U.S. airmen who took their bombs over Nazi territory from a base in England. There, as the film began, the fighting spirit had deteriorated. So a general (Gregory Peck) arrived to take control and to drive the men to greater exertions at a time when they were already exhausted. The general's efforts, conscientious and tough, drained away his own emotional and physical resources; and, for all its patriotic caution, the movie impinged as a stringent study of wartime ethics and morale, implying that deeds extolled as heroic can easily leave permanent scars upon the spirit of man.

Obviously, this anti-heroic trend was not approved by all: especially not by those who had to put up the money and wrinkle their brows over the problem of getting it back. John Huston began to direct *The Red Badge of Courage* (1951) but surrendered the task to others, eventually, when he found it impossible to bring his ideas into line with the requirements of M-G-M, a studio whose patriotism had been emphasised as McCarthyism spread its net to Hollywood. *The Red Badge of Courage,* from the novel by Stephen Crane, was set in the past. The old war between the states had been a stamping ground for many Hollywood directors. But in the transitional social climate of 1951, it was regarded as a fairly hot potato, because it disputed the validity of war as a solution to political and diplomatic muddles. So the film was undermined in production and given short shrift on release.

In the same year, the more adventurous policy at 20th Century-Fox yielded a portrait of the German field marshal, Rommel (James Mason), which was very different from the same man's Hollywood image as carved by Erich von Stroheim in 1943 for Billy Wilder's diverting old melodrama *Five Graves to Cairo.* Mason's interpretation, in *The Desert Fox,* transformed the enemy heavy into a creditable figure, an adversary to be respected—as indeed he was, by certain military types to whom war is a way of life and a test of manhood. The movie, directed by Henry Hathaway, was an adventure yarn which could have been said to glorify war but granted a lot of the glory to an erstwhile enemy. Not erstwhile enough, perhaps: the battle of El Alamein was too recent a piece of history, and many resented this apparent esteem for yesterday's villains. Beneath that

72

kind of surface reaction, there lurked the uncomfortable thought that if only the militarists of opposing sides could have been introduced before hostilities began, and given some toy soldiers and a big relief map to play with, they might have got along so well in harmless competition that life-and-death fighting would have struck them as rather unsporty: in which case, the politicians must surely have been compelled to reach terms without violence. But of course, another thought lurked deeper still: the commanders probably liked the whiff of death, and their game was choice to them because of the violence it required. The audiences for *The Desert Fox* were bound to have contained a quantity of ex-servicemen who had experienced some part of the Second World War, and many who had relatives fighting in Korea. What they saw would understandably hurt them; and it is significant that when Mason played Rommel again for the same studio, in *The Desert Rats* (1952, Robert Wise), the field marshal had become a less engaging figure, no longer valiant but positively ruthless.

So even 20th Century-Fox conformed a bit as the first awkward years of the decade brought their pressures to bear. Spies, however, were another matter entirely: villains or heroes by tradition, depending upon which side they represented (ours or the enemy's), they invariably had a romantic aura. Their reality was of necessity obscure. They were secret people, and therefore intriguing. They caused death, to be sure, but their sneaky activities were usually depicted as quite separate from the unpleasant stench of battle. So Mason and Fox were both on safer ground with *Five Fingers* (1952, Joseph L. Mankiewicz), a deft and satirical thriller based on the true case of the spy known as "Cicero" whose suave operations in Ankara during the early Forties were depicted in such a way as to win a certain admiration for the man's cool courtship with danger, while the money he gained from the sale of top secrets aroused grudging envy in the law-abiding spectator. The oblique comment upon the absurdities which are promoted by conflicting nations braced the romanticism with a cynical wit. The tone was just about right. Unalleviated romanticism would hardly have been apt for a public mindful of the long-winded Alger Hiss case which had contributed to national unrest in the Forties, and to the suspicious ambiance in which McCarthyism thrived.

The cynicism was salutary. So was the black comedy of Billy Wilder's

Stalag 17 (1953), a singularly sophisticated movie from Paramount, where Wilder made a number of his trenchant assaults upon accepted values in society. There were some who took *Stalag 17* quite seriously: probably the same people who had viewed *Five Fingers* with straight faces. At root, these films were dealing with very serious matters. But the treatment was worldly. *Stalag 17* originated as a Broadway play by Edmund Trzcinski and Donald Devan, attuned to the sharp minds among New York theatregoers. It was opened out for cinema to provide spare glimpses of action beyond the confines of a hut to which prisoners of war had been taken by the Germans. But even the exteriors were bleak and grey, befitting the subject and at the same time relating the whole work to normal concepts of film realism. This, as distinct from the discreet sheen of the cinematography in *Five Fingers,* did not induce an immediate tendency to laugh, and so the dark and vigorous humour came as a shock. *Stalag 17* was the very opposite of the familiar thesis established by wartime prison-camp movies, which constantly made the upbeat point that duress brings out the best in a man: here we were asked to realise that it would have been more likely to have brought out the worst. In the claustrophobic hut, the prisoners were shown as a non-heroic bunch. Hardened by war, the GI played by William Holden made a wry contrast to stereotyped Hollywood soldiers; and of the other men who shared his hard and frightened little segment of space in a maddening world, there was only one who measured up to the traditional concept of spruce rectitude. It was no great surprise to those who caught the bitter essence of the movie that this paragon among swine turned out in the end to be a Nazi spy in their midst.

The soldiers of *Stalag 17* were forerunners of the characters who would proliferate more than a decade later in American movies, when the Vietnam war effort was strongly opposed by numerous members of another generation, reacting against the values their parents had been conditioned to accept, and giving rise to films which denigrated war in forthright terms. The satirical method would flourish, for example, in 1970 with Robert Altman's M*A*S*H: and one can detect an affinity with the famous sequence of *Stalag 17,* considered outrageous in its day, where the imprisoned Americans looked through a makeshift spyglass upon some Russian women who had been captured by the Germans and obliged to strip completely for delousing, a spectacle greeted with whoops of lust by the inmates of the hut.

A little later in 1953, with the ground prepared to this extent, came the first major breakthrough in the anti-war films of the Fifties: Fred Zinnemann's *From Here to Eternity,* a diluted but still pungent adaptation of the novel by James Jones. Set, and partially filmed, in and around Hawaii's Schofield Barracks, the movie dealt with corruption in the military way of life during the period of peacetime training for possible combat in 1941, climaxed by the unexpected Japanese attack on Pearl Harbor in December of that year. The issue to emerge most forcefully in the film was militarism's demeanment of the individual, epitomised by the interior acting of Montgomery Clift as Private Prewitt, sinewy and stubborn, perpetually tormented by the thick-set stalwarts of the boxing squad he refused to join, despite his known ability in the ring. Prewitt's symbolic determination not to fight had a psychological base: it was the traumatic result of accidentally killing a close friend with a perfectly judged but fatal right cross in a thoroughly sporting contest. The army officer who commanded him at Schofield was less concerned with the likelihood of war than with the kudos of a championship win for his squad. The metaphor became the focal point of the movie. Prewitt, the non-violent individual in a militant herd, grew weaker and weaker under physical and psychological assault. At the officer's bidding, Prewitt was punished upon every slightest pretext. If he did not commit a misdemeanour, he had to be tricked into doing so. His army life became a constant degradation as he marched or ran under the weight of punitive burdens, or scrubbed floors and washed stacks of crockery, under the sadistic eyes of his tormentors. Throughout all this, Clift's determined yet vulnerable face was eloquent of suffering.

Other debilitating aspects of the isolated army community were noted in excursions beyond the barracks, where the orderly ruthlessness of the men had its repercussions in the behaviour of women. The officer with the boxing fixation had a frustrated wife: a character seized upon with gratitude by Deborah Kerr who until then had been regarded by Hollywood as the quintessence of British refinement. Now, in a black but decorously skirted swimsuit (considered pretty daring in 1953), she partnered the muscular Burt Lancaster in a love scene that provoked sensation (and ripe satire in one of Billy

Wilder's daydream sequences for *The Seven Year Itch* in 1955). On a deserted beach, the unhappy woman and the First Sergeant (whose own deference to army rules was an expedience, foreign to his true nature) strived towards a measure of affirmation in sex. The release of emotions, long restricted by necessary disciplines, was attained with difficulty—nicely indicated by Zinnemann. Lush background music gave place to the soft crashing of surf as he berated her for taking previous lovers. His condonement of convention was ironic. The woman defended herself vehemently against these reproaches, her self-pity aligned with her anger. Their mutual need found physical expression in the classic embrace on the wet sand, the waves lapping towards their bodies. Another woman on the periphery of military events was a prostitute (Donna Reed), known as "The Princess" on account of her haughtiness, dutiful and yet somewhat disdainful as she went about her work in a quaintly improbable brothel called The New Congress Club. In contrast to the discontented matron on the beach, "The Princess" yearned for conformity: "I want to be proper—because when you're proper, you're safe." Hers was the least convincing portion of an otherwise powerful film, but there was as much irony in her ethos as Hollywood could permit itself. The entire movie, visually sharp, had a sourness befitting its progressive attitude.

Interestingly, and to some degree indicative of the "freedom of speech" inheritance, maintained in the face of witch hunting and patriotic pressures, the U.S. Army gave some assistance in the making of *From Here to Eternity*. Likewise the Navy was persuaded by Stanley Kramer to help with his production of *The Caine Mutiny* (1954), another criticism of the serviceman's condition, although in this instance the balance was slightly redressed by the final denunciation of a very ambiguous villain, Lt. Keefer (Fred MacMurray, giving an excellent performance). Keefer's intellectual prowess was coupled to an emotional distaste for service life, verging upon neurosis; also his behaviour could have been equated with an extreme left-wing threat to democracy. In the structure of the screenplay, sympathies were manipulated very smoothly. Keefer seemed to have justice on

Opposite: the beach scene of FROM HERE TO ETERNITY (above) provoked ripe satire (below) in THE SEVEN YEAR ITCH

his side when he pointed out to a fellow officer and an ensign aboard the minesweeper Caine that their new captain, Queeg (Humphrey Bogart), was behaving in the manner of a paranoiac. Queeg, in fact, was a pathetic victim of combat fatigue. His initial impact upon the officers and men of the Caine had been bracing. Then it became disturbing. An obsessive stickler for discipline, Queeg was compulsively disguising his inner sense of dread, which he was incapable of acknowledging even to himself. He was seen to be afraid and inadequate as a commander when faced with enemy fire or with the problem of navigating his battered vessel through a typhoon. His behaviour, and Keefer's insidious opposition to him, gave an executive officer the impression (probably correct in the circumstances) that there was no alternative to arresting the captain and taking over command. Hence the subsequent charge of mutiny.

The film was a neat compromise between elaborate production and calculated plotting, well directed by Edward Dmytryk and based on the long novel by Herman Wouk, who had already compressed its essential points into a gripping stage play called *The Caine Mutiny Court Martial*. In the cinema too it was the court martial sequence (comparatively succinct because we had been shown the events that led to it) that made the strongest impression, due in no small measure to Bogart's intelligent acting as Queeg. His assurance at the start of his interrogation was steadily undermined by the counsel for the defence of the "mutineers" (Jose Ferrer), a navy man, dutiful in his immediate task, and yet inwardly compassionate towards Queeg. His legal tactics broke Queeg's fragile mask of normality. Bogart's voice rose hysterically in self-justification, and then came abruptly to a stop, while the camera trapped him in an enormous close-up: a picture of sudden self-awareness, in a silence filled with tension for Queeg himself and for those who witnessed his shame.

The nature of that shame had been symbolised bluntly, throughout the film and especially during the trial, by Queeg's habit of taking a pair of steel ball bearings from his pocket and rolling them mindlessly in the palm of his hand: knowing that his fear could lead to the social stigma of cowardice, he clung unconsciously to a token of manhood. The equivocal state of the conformist mind in the Fifties had a diverting reflection in advertisements inserted in magazines by a fun-and-games firm, suggesting that their latest line, "Queeg-balls,"

Inner sense of dread—Van Johnson as the executive officer and Humphrey Bogart as Queeg in THE CAINE MUTINY

would make a nice present for paranoid friends.

Keefer's resentment and spite on the one hand, and Queeg's self-reproach on the other, were astute devices to show how far the individual personality can be driven in the unnatural sphere of war. Steadily, through courageous and telling movies amid the continuing flow of glamour, Hollywood depicted the anomalies of service life. One of the Hollywood-abroad epics, *The Bridge on the River Kwai* (1957), had as its central figure the ludicrous and pathetic Colonel Nicholson (Alec Guinness). David Lean's neat direction of the movie, strong on emotive imagery as weary prisoners marched gamely to their whistling of "Colonel Bogey," still left spectators a choice of reactions. What the subject needed was something like the black satire of *Stalag 17*. What it promoted, at first, was sympathy for Colonel Nicholson when, in a sequence of perfectly straight drama, he was put to torture (confined to a claustrophobic hot box) by his Japanese captors in 1943. From there on, the general tendency was to take the movie straight, although it was replete with derisive irony. Based on a novel by Pierre Boulle, who had been a prisoner of the Japanese himself, its historic background was the building of the notorious "death railway" in Siam. To form an important part of this railway, the Japanese commandant (Sessue Hayakawa) ordered his prisoners to build a substantial bridge across the River Kwai. Nicholson, holding

A potentially hilarious compromise—Sessue Hayakawa and Alec Guinness in THE BRIDGE ON THE RIVER KWAI

to his ingrained notions of propriety, refused to let his officers do such work alongside enlisted men. In a potentially hilarious compromise, the commandant (a former foreign student at the London Polytechnic) applied diplomacy to the situation in accordance with British modes of thought, while at the same time saving face in the oriental style by using the anniversary of an ancient Japanese victory as an excuse to be magnanimous and agree to the Colonel's request. So the British officers were excused from manual labour. In the meantime, the prisoners at work on the bridge were sabotaging the operation constantly, and no sooner had one section been constructed than it fell down in a shambles. Once the Colonel had been given his way, however, he became obsessed with the idea of doing the job properly, as a discipline, and also as a testament to British fortitude and workmanship: a thorough and efficient military operation, regardless of the fact that it would be a great help to the enemy. In a parallel plot, an American sailor (William Holden), at the behest of a British major in Ceylon (Jack Hawkins), led a commando party on a mission to destroy the bridge. This was done, in the impressively ironic climax, bringing to ruins the work that Colonel Nicholson had supervised with such absurd pride. "Madness, madness," cried a British medical officer at the end—and indeed it was, although the movie as a whole (due in part to the fine, but possibly too "straight" acting of Guinness) sustained an excess of sympathy for the Colonel. Pierre Boulle had described this character as an "example of 'the Indian Army officer,' a type considered legendary" who provokes in those around him "alternating bouts of anger and affection." If pathos were more evident than madness in the long run, the Colonel's instinctive obedience to his own militaristic code had the saving grace of a similarity to the valid therapy of keeping busy, doing anything to hand, rather than moping in times of trouble. The film's producer, Sam Spiegel, gave a shrewd assessment of the theme: "Man came into this world to build, and not to destroy. Yet he's thrown into the necessity of destroying, and his one everlasting instinct is to try to save himself from having to destroy." Looking at *The Bridge on the River Kwai* from this point of view, the ending is closer to tragedy than to satire.

The entire idea of military training and discipline was called into question in another Spiegel production, *The Strange One* (also 1957), directed by Jack Garfein, and adapted for the screen by Calder Willingham from his own novel and stage play *End as a Man* (this title was resumed for the movie's U.K. release). Set in a military academy in the U.S.A. (Willingham himself had undergone some training at such an establishment), it implied that its chief villain, a sadistic young cadet (Ben Gazzara) was an odd case who would have proved corrupt in any environment but was nurtured in evil by the academy's methods. Fiercely the movie refuted the glamourised image of cadets, and the implicit admiration of their disciplinary years. The glamour was still being perpetuated elsewhere, because the variety of Fifties cinema was infinite. John Ford's *The Long Gray Line* (1955), all sweetness and sunlight, glorified West Point. And the dining hall habits depicted in that sorry film, from such a great director, were bemusingly reminiscent of the routines endured by "cadet" Dick Powell in *Flirtation Walk,* a musical of the Thirties that took its title from the Academy's decorous lover's lane. There it had been Powell's lot to sit rigid at table, eating to orders barked by a uniformed superior, tucking in his chin, raising a food-laden fork from the plate in a strictly vertical movement until it was parallel with his mouth and then bringing it smartly towards its destination at an angle of ninety degrees. He ended as a man, we gathered (although he appeared to be trained as a robot), and he sang the title song to Ruby Keeler in a glossy finale that condoned the venerable traditions. Things were certainly very different in the Willingham view. The subservience imposed upon newcomers by those of higher rank in *The Strange One* was not seen as a salutary thing, but as a tempting chance for the cruel streak in the superior to assert itself. One specific enormity was the application of an enema, filled with hard liquor, to contaminate the bloodstream of a recruit who was left to lie outdoors all night and be expelled for drunken misbehaviour: a lucky victim, one felt—well out of it all.

Nevertheless, cheek by jowl with such eyebrow-raisers, the notion that submission to a virtually dehumanising discipline could be beneficial, to a man and to his country, was widely held. Hollywood acknowledged this more than once. In muddlesome ambiguity, a comedy intended primarily as entertainment, *The Girl He Left Behind* (1956, David Butler), obliged the clean-cut Tab Hunter to toe the militaristic line with pride . . but only just in time for the fade-out.

All through the movie his attitude had been that of a maverick: a revolt against the peacetime army's intrusion upon his individuality. He was a spoiled boy, to be sure, but he was manfully embarrassed by the silver-spooning thrust upon him by a doting mother (Jessie Royce Landis). Removed from affluent freedom to spartan barracks, he eschewed the camaraderie of army life, withdrawing into spiritual isolation, lying upon his bunk in off-duty periods, ignoring the others and hoping they would be good enough to ignore him too. They didn't. They detested him, and they let him know it. Nevertheless he saved the life of one of them during grenade training: a nervous trainee did the wrong thing, and our anti-hero leapt to the rescue with the reflex-agility of the college football whizzkid he used to be. Complimented by one and all for his "heroism" in averting what might have been a fatality, and possibly several fatalities, he declared with bared teeth, "I only did it to save the life of someone near and dear to me. Me." This, bear in mind, was a comedy. One warmed to the character. But the joke wore thin, and simultaneously it became clear that he would end up by heeding the advice of an older man (who had found in the army a salvation from a lifetime of not "belonging"): "You ought to stop being a loner." God help the kid, he did more than that. By fade-out time he had assumed the demeanour of sadistic authoritarianism, meting out to new recruits the very treatment he had resented so much himself at the beginning, and marching with head high to martial music in the movie's volte-face finale. He had been more likable by far at the point where he was solemnly threatened with discharge "under conditions other than honourable," to which he replied, "Sir, I have just one question. How soon?"

Conversely, it was argued as always that individuality was often equivalent to selfishness and that life within any society requires personal discipline. True as this is, the matter is one of degree: never easy to convey dramatically to audiences who are believed to prefer the issues cut and dried, and the endings conclusive. In respect of war, embarked upon because of diplomatic failure, the individual had the right to declare himself a conscientious objector. In the Fifties, it was still considered deplorable to make this kind of stand: a refuge for cowards, in the general view, unless a strong religious belief supported an individual's abstention; and even that was usually regarded

*Religiously bound to refrain—Gary Cooper,
Richard Eyer and Anthony Perkins in FRIENDLY
PERSUASION*

as quirky. The predicament of Quakers, religiously bound to refrain
from violence, was pertinently expounded in William Wyler's *Friendly
Persuasion* (1956). Although the story was set in the past, the meaning
was contemporary. Korean veterans and their wives and families were
in the audience now. The plot concerned an uninvolved family of
the Quaker faith, living in the southern part of Indiana and threatened
by invasion. As head of the family, Gary Cooper voiced the opinion
that other means than violence should be found to arrange matters
compatibly between the opposing sides. But violence was seen as an
inherent flaw in human nature, not to be subdued beneath a show
of civilisation.

Hollywood had progressed sufficiently to inveigh against the Korean

Karl Malden directing Dolores Michaels and Richard Widmark on the set of TIME LIMIT

involvement with *Time Limit* (1957, an excursion into directing by Karl Malden, one of the very few actors who did well in this capacity). *Time Limit* was adapted from a Broadway play about the mysterious refusal of a major (Richard Basehart) to defend himself against charges of giving information to the Communists while they held him prisoner. In structure, it resembled a thriller, reaching a sensational denouement when one of the major's fellow prisoners (Rip Torn), now also returned to the U.S.A., broke down under questioning and unfolded a disturbing story, about the culpability of a dead captain who had been imprisoned with them. Hitherto, this dead man had been assumed by the U.S. authorities to be the solitary hero in the midst of rogues, but in fact he was the only prisoner who had collaborated with the enemy, and for that reason he had been killed by his own countrymen in the prison camp. Consequently, they had all been threatened with execution by the Japanese commandant, and only then did the major agree to collaborate in order to save their lives. Before returning home, the men had agreed upon a conspiracy of silence to protect the major from punishment, or possibly death, at the hands of their own people. The dilemma was acute: the major had saved a handful of men he knew, by giving information which would cause the deaths of many others he did not know personally. The human element weighed more strongly in this individual than the virtually abstract demand of duty. The machine-tooled theatrical origin of the piece was evident, but it did crystallise the wartime pressures. It was a powerful anti-war statement, in effect. Dialogue and acting were notably strong, especially in the portrayal of the major's bewildered wife (June Lockhart), loving her husband and at the same time, as a conditioned member of society, ashamed of him. *Time Limit* expressed two matters in forthright terms: the Communist assumption that a desired end will justify any means of achieving it, and the human inclination to favour personal friends more than anonymous multitudes. At the end of the film, the major agreed to face a court martial, ruefully wondering if it could possibly lead to a satisfactory answer to his problems. His interrogator (Richard Widmark), who after tough work and shrewd psychology had arrived at the truth and, knowing it, had decided to act as counsel for the major's defence, gave the movie its final potent punch: "I'll promise you one thing, Major. They'll know we asked the questions."

The ending is not inadequate, but honest: no neat conclusion, but a challenge to each spectator, a questioning of values. Movies that began to make us ask ourselves questions were on the side of civilisation. Some of the avowedly anti-war movies were of an equivocal nature. It was debatable whether their graphic battle sequences aroused the inherent violence of certain spectators, rather than assuaging the violent urge through a vicarious kick. The same thing could be said of violence in thrillers, but there is a significant difference: the brutality in thrillers is usually illegal, whereas in war movies the physical conflict is legalised. The impact of violence in cinema is greater, of course, when it involves only two people as distinct from the mass action of war movies from which a director might pluck occasional close shots of horrific detail to make the human suffering impinge from the swirling anonymity of spectacular long-shots. There was surely no impact of violence in the Hollywood Fifties to equal the two tremendous shocks in Fritz Lang's thriller *The Big Heat* (1953) when Lee Marvin disfigured Gloria Graham by hurling some hot coffee in her face, and later when she retaliated in kind. Considered in isolation, such palpable violence would be highly suspect. Contained as it was by a sharp little plot and sensible psychology, as well as the brilliant light-and-shadow play which typified the high style of Lang at his post-expressionist best, even in these dog days of his Hollywood career, the sensation was justifiable and possibly, for some, cathartic. In the work of Fritz Lang at this period one found the good things of the Hollywood Forties, still vibrant. But they were giving place to a new breed of stylist whose toughness belonged to a worldwide change in filmic values, which became apparent to Hollywood by the end of the decade. A new feeling for the medium was in the air. It lurked, ready to emerge later, in the underground cinema of New York, regarded by Hollywood as negligible then. And it put its foot firmly in Hollywood's guarded door when Stanley Kubrick made *The Killing* (1956). Here was a fairly new director, with another thriller: a nimble plot about a racetrack robbery, succinct and credible in its character drawing, but above all progressive in its style. Naturally the thriller, a *genre* so malleable to the cinema's versatile techniques, was a safe commercial prospect. Kubrick's freshness was due in part to his apparent assimilation of precepts. Several times, the same passage of action was repeated from the viewpoint of different characters, in a compression of the form chosen by Orson Welles in 1941 for *Citizen Kane*. The violence of *The Killing* was not condoned by Kubrick: the characters were understandable but unsympathetic. The following year on location in Germany, Kubrick had substantial Hollywood finance for *Paths of Glory* (1957), the bravest anti-war movie of the decade. Again the style had precepts. The superb black-and-white cinematography by Georg Krause and the emphatic compositions ordained by Kubrick, with figures related dramatically to their backgrounds in trenches or palatial castles, carried memories of Lang and of Welles. The sweeping camera movement across a battleground was based in classic film

technique. But the style was individual, the work of a young master who understood and applied the fundamentals of his art in a manner distinctly his own.

There was no comfort to be gained, except by the most blinkered of spectators, from the fact that the story belonged to the First World War. *Paths of Glory* indicted corruption among military leaders. Its power came from the more personal fighting of the older war, admittedly easier to illustrate in horrific visuals, but its meaning was apt to any generation of soldiers and their commanders. Calder Willingham was among the screenplay writers, drawing upon a novel by Humphrey Cobb. Personal aggrandisement was the motive of high-ranking French army officers who ordered a reckless charge against superior German forces, and covered up its inevitable failure by having French soldiers court-martialled for cowardice. The obscenity was explicit, in shots of the maimed and the slaughtered, and in the selfish cruelty of the autocrats, who were played by Adolphe Menjou (suave and callous) and George Macready (a portrait of neurosis). These fine and scathing performances carried much weight, throwing sympathy and respect upon Kirk Douglas as the clean-minded colonel who opposed evil with forthright anger.

It was unique among the war films, undoubtedly, and while it raised hackles it certainly appealed to the pacifist strain that began to assert itself slowly in the aftermath of Korea, later to divide the U.S.A. into opposing camps over the troubles in Vietnam. In addition, once McCarthy had fallen, the freedom of speech for which American cinema had always been noted (a freedom rarely matched in Britain, for example, let alone the U.S.S.R.) took a new lease of life. Political satire had been remarkably strong as early as 1953 in *Call Me Madam,* cutting through the jollity of the lightweight Irving Berlin musical (adapted from a Broadway hit with Ethel Merman repeating her stage success, and efficiently directed by Walter Lang). The wisecracks at the expense of President Truman and his family were rather jovial: the movie had a slightly dated quality, because by this time Eisenhower was president; but the picture of a brash American female ambassador, distributing largesse to a fictitious European country ("Can You Use Any Money Today?" was a palpable

Opposite: George Macready and Adolphe Menjou in
PATHS OF GLORY

hit), drew astonishingly trenchant contrast from commercial vulgarity on the one hand and pathetic old-world dignity on the other. It was light, but not trivial. The uncouth assumption that money solved every problem was rigorously lampooned: the U.S.A. frequently usurped the British prerogative of being the land most willing to laugh itself to scorn. This was healthy stuff. However, some of the saucier lyrics were omitted, because Hollywood still languished under an antiquated Production Code that was extremely uptight concerning sex. A formidable assault upon the Code itself, and a flaunting of the powerful Legion of Decency, brought Otto Preminger into the news in the same year as *Call Me Madam,* with his 1953 movie of the 1951 Broadway play *The Moon Is Blue*: in Hollywood's opinion the dialogue was likewise. In fact, even in 1951, sophisticated theatre audiences were given little cause to raise their eyebrows by this mildly entertaining piece, but the movie audience was further-flung and hitherto sheltered from words like "seduction." The movie was even rebuked by Cardinal Spellman. Needless to say, the sheltered masses flocked to see and hear what all the fuss was about, and a pleasant but rather tame little comedy became historic as a major breakthrough against censorship.

After this, the floodgates were open. Inevitably there was an influx of titillating trash, often failing to live up to the promise of the posters but troublesome enough to bring Senator Kefauver to Hollywood to investigate matters. With McCarthy out of its hair, the cinema made short work of other protesting voices. Sex and even violence were hardly to be classed as serious matters by comparison with patriotism. Commerce was strongly on the side of sex, naturally. And, in fact, many good intelligent films gained realism from their sudden freedom in this respect. Any fool could distinguish between the quality and the dross.

Subjects previously noted obliquely in Hollywood films were discussed more openly now, but in most cases with caution, for fear of alienating the sizeable conformist sector of the public. Preminger gained an extra degree of authenticity by including a good deal of sexual detail in the dialogue of his mystery thriller *Anatomy of a Murder* (1959), a film hardly to be put down as prurient since it was taken from a novel by a United States Justice, John D. Voelker (whose book had been published under the pseudonym of Robert

A landmark in permissive cinema—ANATOMY OF A MURDER with James Stewart and Ben Gazzara

Traver, but whose actual name was used freely at the time of filming). Its well-constructed story, intriguing in plot development and keen in characterisation, concerned the trial of an army officer for the murder of a man who might or might not have raped his wife (Lee Remick, splendidly teasing in her restricted portrait of a sexy woman whose real situation had to remain in doubt until the *dénouement*). Using real backgrounds in Michigan, including a courtroom where the camera gyrations nimbly alleviated the long dialogue-reliant passages of the trial, the film had a number of novel and admirable qualities. It used a dramatic jazz score by Duke Ellington; and striking credit titles of a dismembered body, designed by Saul Bass whose work in this line was frequently superior to the movies that followed his introductory credit-sequences. These two elements were fashionable trends of the period, reinforced by the substance of the film as a whole. Moreover, at two hours and forty minutes in black-and-white it made a striking contrast to the glossy blockbusters with its astringent realism. And the cast was formidable: James Stewart for the defence and George C. Scott for the prosecution clashed in courtroom arguments and explicit clinical details; Ben Gazzara was aptly enigmatic as the accused; Arthur O'Connell played a wily attorney, slightly addicted to the bottle; Eve Arden knew, as always, just how far to go with the brittle comic relief as Stewart's secretary; and the judge was beautifully portrayed by Joseph N. Welch (a gentleman of great personal charm and dignity: the Boston attorney who in real life had recently spoken words of history-making condemnation to Senator Joseph McCarthy).

Another drama of 1959 with a climactic courtroom sequence of a notably progressive order was *Compulsion,* which dealt (albeit in terms of psychopathology) with the subject of homosexuality, previously only mentioned or implied in the cloudiest of ways by Hollywood, and then invariably as a matter for disapproval or even ridicule. *Compulsion* was already well known as a book and a stage play, both written by Meyer Levin. It was a dramatic analysis of a notorious murder case of the Twenties. The victim was a boy of fourteen, the killers two highly intelligent university students, Nathan Leopold and Richard Loeb (fictitious names were used in the movie, and the characters were played by Dean Stockwell and Bradford Dillman). Carrying experience to extremes, in fantasies woven wildly around the philosophy of Nietzsche, their sexual relationship took the master-and-slave form and murder was carried out as a triumph of the intellectual mind over the presumably humbler brains devoted to detection. The undoubted insanity of the pair was made clear during the trial, where a powerful speech in favour of leniency was made by Clarence Darrow (Orson Welles). The murderers were given life imprisonment instead of capital punishment; and the denunciation of life-for-a-life barbarism was to become a repeated element in the films of Richard Fleischer, who directed *Compulsion.* The same case had been dramatised for cinema before in Hitchcock's *Rope* (1948) which, as Fleischer remarked, "skirted the issues." Hitchcock had no alternative, of course, in view of the power of censorship at that time. Fleischer had the benefit of the liberality that flourished in the latter half of the Fifties, not without constant outcries great and small. There were many who disapproved of the picture of America

*A master-and-slave relationship—Bradford Dillman
and Dean Stockwell in COMPULSION*

that would be given to countries overseas, and in fact the extreme
left-wing inclination in a number of countries was to point to Hollywood films of this era as evidence of American corruption, over-
looking the point that similar flaws existed in other parts of the
world but that many governments would have suppressed any attempt
to incorporate these social elements in a film.

Abortion was treated with kid gloves in *Blue Denim* (1959, Philip
Dunne: U.K. title, *Blue Jeans*), a disarming little study of 'teenagers
(Carol Lynley and Brandon de Wilde) whose passion had got the
better of them, and whose parents were easily shocked: a minor
airing of a major matter, it holds retrospective interest because it
was based on a play by James Leo Herlihy, whose novels *All Fall
Down* and *Midnight Cowboy* were turned into consequential films of
the Sixties.

Miscegenation, without so much as a physical manifestation of it, was mooted guardedly in *Island in the Sun* (1957, Robert Rossen), with Joan Fontaine nobly tackling the chore of fusing white respectability with human sexuality, and Harry Belafonte as the handsomest black man in the whole wide world. One felt that both of these intelligent performers must have appreciated the whimsicality of their assignments, while perhaps at the same time being glad enough to take a step in the right direction. The segregation of races had been declared unconstitutional in the U.S.A. in 1954, but in many areas no notice was taken of that. Hollywood got around to the subject, typically, by way of the Old West, thinking itself very advanced in 1950 when the Indian as villain was firmly expunged by Jeff Chandler's sympathetic portrayal of the Apache leader, Cochise,

Brandon de Wilde in BLUE DENIM, a study of 'teenagers whose passion got the better of them

94

in *Broken Arrow,* directed by Delmer Daves for (unsurprisingly) 20th Century-Fox.

The attitude was less clear-cut and therefore more persuasive in John Ford's *The Searchers* (1956), with such an established Ford hero-figure as John Wayne playing an embittered Confederate fighter who, after the Civil War, became obsessed with the pursuit of Comanche Indians who had killed some of his kinsfolk and had abducted two girls. John Ford was having a decade of peaks and chasms: this was one of the peaks. It qualified his familiar style by introducing the racial element rather subtly into a typical Ford balance between the tough and the sentimental. His familiar stamping ground of Monument Valley in Utah, with its spatial grandeur and its majestic flat-topped rock formations, took on a fresh splendour in VistaVision, and Ford caught on quickly to the idea of putting a camera inside a room and opening a door upon the sunlit vastness, creating a frame within a frame, a shadowy surround with a grand but dangerous territory beyond. "Shall We Gather at the River?" was sung. "The Yellow Rose of Texas" was played at a dance: all the Ford things happened in the way his admirers had come to expect. But, in addition, the dignity of the Indians with their separate code, and the persistent vengeance of the Wayne character whose conventions were shaken by the discovery that the one kidnapped girl who survived (Natalie Wood) had become adjusted to her status as a squaw, brought the film well within the Fifties belt of social comment, relevant to the time in which it was made, despite the fact that its story was set in the latter part of the Nineteenth century.

But the Indian of the past and his descendants on their segregated reservations were easier to look upon with friendship than the black Americans, those erstwhile figures of Hollywood fun or occasional pathos. To whites they constituted a half-recognised rebuke. There was shame for the whites in the background of black slavery; there was also, it was whispered, a deal of truth to the rumour that black males were decidedly more virile than whites, and black women more ardent. The psychological tensions were possibly greater than the social connotations. Therefore *Island in the Sun,* recognised as a compromise when it was new, was nonetheless a slight advance. And *Edge of the City* (1957, Martin Ritt: U.K. title, *A Man Is Ten Feet Tall*), while also a compromise, was a marginally greater advance.

*White weakness, black strength—John Cassavetes and
Sidney Poitier in EDGE OF THE CITY*

Stanley Kramer's *The Defiant Ones* (1958) was a giant step forward.

The crudeness of *Edge of the City* was in its over-simplified story. Its good intentions carried it away. Yet, in its time, it showed courage. One of Hollywood's pickups from television, the expanded screenplay by Robert Alan Aurthur presented a white neurotic (John Cassavetes) who had weathered a problem childhood, and had deserted from the army. He still harboured a nagging guilt about his brother's death. His character delineation was like a roll-call of all the familiar psychiatric hang-ups that movies usually confronted one at a time. As a manual labourer, he was befriended by a black co-worker (Sidney Poitier) who saw life as a thing of joy and attempted to redeem the white man. In a melodramatic climax, involving a vicious fight with hooks between the Cassavetes character and a bullying foreman, Poitier saved his friend's life but died in the struggle. Despite its heavy demarcation between white weakness and black strength, it was an extremely well made film. Its producer, David Susskind, a television producer of note, appreciated the difference in media: "We tore up the TV script and began again, because the television project was inhibited—to be done in a studio. We wrote another script, we hope we enriched the characters and expanded their geography and their horizon. We went on location in the railroad yards and around the city of New York. We tried to visualise it far and away over what we had done as a television show." At the same time, Susskind attributed Hollywood's new-found racial conscience to business acumen: "What drove them to it was a frenzied search for material that would galvanise the public. They felt that if they dealt with themes that had never been dealt with before, maybe that would get the public to come to the movies."

Several years after the film had been shown, Sidney Poitier took issue with me when I told him I considered the concept artificial: "No, it was not. The character I played was symbolic of what people would like to be. He was not a black character or a white character: he was all characters, you see. He was the man that all people can look upon and wish they were like. He was a strong man. He was a just man. He was a well-loved man. He was a happy full-of-life man. He spread love and glad tidings wherever he moved. Everyone would like to be like that. And these ingredients of his character made his colour invisible. The white man again was symbolic. The white world oftimes carries a false image of itself, because there is no one with a voice of authority to censure it. So the image it has of itself is the image it wishes to create—the exact image that the *black* character represented. The white world, being permitted to create its own image, oftimes creates an image very unlike what its real disposition is. Are you following me?" I was; but what he was saying didn't come across that way, to me, in the film. Poitier's enthusiasm for *Edge of the City* was the more impressive because he felt very strongly that many previous Hollywood portraits of black Americans had been artificial: "I've made an awful lot of them, so I'll name ones I was in: *All the Young Men,* for instance." (1960, Hall Bartlett). "Successful at the box-office but horrifyingly one-dimensional: it wasn't intended to be but it turned out to be. And *Red Ball Express.*"

(1952, Budd Boetticher). "An army film—*another* army film—bad film. I've done many one-dimensional bad films like that. Now, to film-makers, the Negro is not an oddity. He's not a rarity. They see him every day. They live in the same towns with him. Yet they put him on the screen in a saintly unreal manner, because the Negro must represent a certain kind of character in order to help the white man absolve himself of certain guilt feelings and attitudes. They feel they have in their hands the authority and the ability to determine what a film will do. So they say, 'Well now, I'm going to make a wonderful humane statement with the presence of this Negro person who has lived under great handicaps and great denial all of his life.' So they make a statement. And the statement finally is, 'You should be nice to your coloured friends. They too are human beings.' Well, this is messy, you know. That's why the black characters usually come out on the screen as saints, as the other-cheek-turners, as people who are not really people: who are so nice and good. It's messy. As a matter of fact, I'm just dying to play villains."

Beneath Poitier's acting, and that of John Cassavetes, and the undeniable cinematic style of *Edge of the City,* it seemed to me that the black character, albeit symbolic, was precisely the one-dimensional saint that he agreed was false in the majority of films made in the latter part of the Fifties. Symbolic again, but with verisimilitude, not only strength but white-hating anger, was the black convict of Stanley Kramer's *The Defiant Ones,* also played by Poitier: "That was one of the exceptions. Probably *the* one. Stanley Kramer is a man, a producer, marked by his search for the truth. However, Stanley Kramer stands pretty much alone in the film industry."

Kramer had taken over direction, by this time, of the films he produced, and *The Defiant Ones* was a peak in his career. Photographed in monochrome, discreetly stylised in many of its visuals, it symbolised the black-white antagonism by literally shackling Cullen (Poitier) to the Caucasian Jackson (Tony Curtis). Both men were in a prison van, manacled together by iron bands on their wrists and a strong chain stretching four feet at its fullest extension, linking them and aggravating their hatred of one another—a hatred based instinctively on skin tones, white and black. At night on a dark road, the van driver swerved to avoid a collision and ran the vehicle down an incline. It overturned. A close-up filled the screen: one heavy tyre of the van slowly revolving under the rain. Time was passing. By the time the lawmen and the newsmen had gathered, Cullen and Jackson had vanished. This was the south, and the hunt was on. "How come they chained a white man to a black?" asked a reporter, and the sheriff of the area replied, "The warden's got a sense of humour."

On the run, the two men had a mutual need but no *rapport*. They had to cross a river, the water running fast in a frame filled only by its torrent and the chain stretched in the foreground, a white hand on the left edge of the screen, a black hand on the right. In the rapids, the black man went under, but Jackson dragged him ashore. "Thanks for pulling me out," said Cullen. "Man, I didn't pull you out," said Jackson, "I stopped you from pulling me in." The sharp, heightened dialogue by Nathan E. Douglas and Harold Jacob Smith gradually modified the vituperation. Jackson began by calling Cullen "Nigger" and eased off to "Boy" which was not well received either. In the course of their adventures—for this was a suspenseful chase film and the police were after them with dogs—they came upon a small settlement at dead of night. Ironically, Cullen gave Jackson some mud to blacken his face as they ventured among the buildings: "Your white face—it shines out like a clear moon. Don't take it wrong." They ran into trouble there, and were almost lynched by the bigoted townsfolk. But one of their number (Lon Chaney) talked the others down. The group disbanded, leaving a small fire in the centre of the frame, a fire which steadily died while a grey dawn light carried time forward: this virtually theatrical effect, sparingly applied in one or two other phases of the movie, served as a gentle reminder of the symbolism intended while the characters repeatedly behaved as individuals. The man who had spoken up on their behalf came at first light to cut the ropes that bound them to a post, and let them go. As his hand went expertly about his work, they noted on his wrists the indentations of manacles similar to the ones they wore themselves. And now their run was resumed, in visuals of balletic grace as the binding chain and the changing relationship brought a unity to their progress. This was not sustained, however. They quarreled again, and, in a tremendous passage of violence and sorrow, they fought, each dealing blows with one free hand. A woman be-friended them eventually: long deserted by her husband, seeing in

*A giant step forward for racial drama—Sidney
Poitier and Tony Curtis in THE DEFIANT ONES*

Jackson an escape from her solitary life, and breaking the chain to
let Cullen go his own way, directing him towards quicksands to
prevent him from telling possible captors where Jackson had gone.
When Jackson discovered this treachery, he left the woman and went
after Cullen. But Jackson was ill now, impeding Cullen's progress.
The black man exhorted him to keep going: "You're dragging on the
chain." The chain was a thing of the past, but its purpose had been
served. The police closed in, and Cullen might easily have evaded
them but he waited instead, with Jackson faint in his arms; and when
the sheriff walked right up to them and saw the way things were,
he put away his gun.

If sentiment often bordered upon sentimentality in *The Defiant*

Ones, Kramer and his players knew just how far to let it ride, just when to rein it in. Among the racial dramas of the Fifties, this was by far the best.

The one aspect of sociology that Hollywood did not tend to handle with caution was the media menace. Obviously it cocked a snook whenever possible at television; sometimes gawkily, as in the film version of the Broadway comedy *Will Success Spoil Rock Hunter?* (1957, Frank Tashlin manfully directing material unworthy of his talents: U.K. title, *Oh for a Man!*). It burlesqued the brain-washing commercials, among other things, and the best laugh it raised came during the credit titles when a girl was seen with an active washing machine, extolling its powers while desperately trying to extricate a pair of trousers from its tenacious interior and being hauled into the cauldron herself. If the manner was generally too broad, the reproaches against gullibility and the readiness of communication outlets to exploit the susceptible *en masse* were part of a useful trend, which had been evident in a desultory way for quite some time.

The opportunist news-reporter was derided, along with public insensitivity, by Billy Wilder's *The Big Carnival* (1951, U.K. title *Ace in the Hole*). In a terse screenplay, written by Wilder in collaboration with Lesser Samuels and Walter Newman, Chuck Tatum (Kirk Douglas) was a reporter who awaited a scoop that would give him bigtime circulation. In desert country, bored at the prospect of covering a rattlesnake hunt, he happened upon a small group of people, gathered beside a mountain. A woman informed him that her husband, who had been looking for Indian relics, was trapped inside the mountain by a sudden cave-in. Tatum managed to talk to the man, and ordered his young photographer to get busy with pictures. Tatum's idea was to keep the man incarcerated for as long as possible, and thereby to build himself a story. Trippers began to gather, to gawk at the Mountain of the Seven Vultures about which they had read so much in the press, and to contemplate the rescue work in progress—a progress which Tatum deliberately slowed down, by promising the local sheriff advantageous publicity at election time if he would be so kind as to abandon the fairly rapid work of shoring up the cliff walls and adopt the longer method of drilling through from the top of the mountain. A carnival grew up around the spreading crowd. The game continued until Tatum realised that the man in the cave was on the point of death: only then did he begin to hate himself.

Under the sunbaked rock, Wilder's carnival was a chilling spectacle. Thematically it was perhaps of minority influence, and the same could be said of *The Great Man* (1957), directed by Jose Ferrer who also played the lead, a hack-man at a radio station, assigned to compile a memorial programme about a widely revered broadcaster whose death brought multitudes to the Yankee Stadium where the body was lying in state. Darting among them with a recorder, Ferrer obtained trivial comments from which a technician edited a tape-montage, blending phrases and even single words into a composite impression of heart-felt mourning. Then, proceeding to interview people who had known the revered deceased, Ferrer learned that the man he was to eulogise had been, in fact, an unscrupulous opportunist, using everyone who befriended him as a stepping-stone to personal advancement. This was hardly a movie to stand the test of time. Its style was almost constantly reminiscent of television, with most shots at very close range and an improbably optimistic ending in which the hack-man threw away his script at the microphone and told listeners the truth about their dead idol. In its day, it had a certain bite; yet in the same year Elia Kazan bit harder with *A Face in the Crowd,* the ferocious tragi-comedy of Lonesome Rhodes (Andy Griffith), discovered in an Arkansas jail by a radio reporter (Patricia Neal, an actress to make the utmost of every nuance). She persuaded Lonesome to play the guitar and to sing for her listeners, and, once out of prison, he was headed for a media career, first in radio and then on TV, singing songs and plugging pills and giving little homespun chats which earned him enormous popularity. The movie, from a Budd Schulberg story, made it clear that Lonesome was on the make from the very beginning: "What do I get out of this, me, myself and I?" When millions began to admire him, and the financial rewards mounted, he tasted power and liked the savour. Kazan showed him, to be sure, looking down from his New York penthouse upon a vista of TV aerials and feeling afraid. But this was fleeting: stronger in his mind was the knowledge that he had become "not just an entertainer . . a force." Indeed, he was a megalomaniac: "This whole country's just like my flock of sheep. . . . hillbillies, hausfraus. . . . everybody that's got to jump when somebody else blows a whistle. . . . THEY'RE MINE." The woman who had started him on this heady course, and

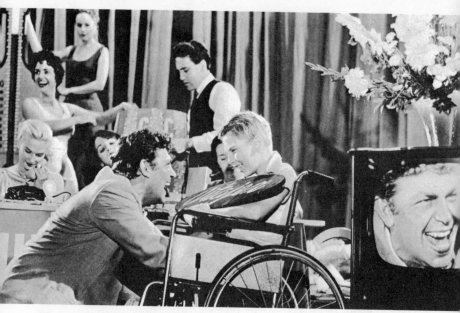

The megalomania of Lonesome Rhodes—Andy Griffith in A FACE IN THE CROWD

wavered by his side compassionately as she saw it get out of hand, finally knew that it was her responsibility now to destroy him. Her strategy was to flip a control-room switch to let the public hear what Lonesome Rhodes was apt to say when his programme had finished and he thought they weren't listening. His fall was heavy, because he had grown pretty big: it was a warning to the easily seduced, a token of the cinema's social awareness, a watchdog of a satire that left toothmarks wherever it was seen.

103

5. Individuals or Misfits?

IN HENRY HATHAWAY'S *Fourteen Hours* (1950), Richard Base-hart played a man who stood indecisively upon the ledge of a building, high above an impersonal city, resisting efforts by friends and police to lure him back, and yet unable to make the suicidal leap. It was a comparatively modest psychological drama, an echo of similar instances from real life. It prefigured a theme that persisted significantly throughout the decade: the plight of the individual who cannot adjust. He might be an exceptional victim of circumstance, like the man mistakenly accused of a crime he did not commit in Alfred Hitchcock's *The Wrong Man* (1957), a specific case taken from life and treated by Hitchcock in an untypical semi-documentary style which concentrated upon the helpless sensation that overwhelmed this guiltless victim (Henry Fonda); and, as evidence mounted to condemn him, we were shown the side effect, the dreadful mental strain upon his wife (Vera Miles) who, after trying every possible means of establishing his innocence, lapsed into a state of apathy. This woman's condition was perhaps one of the most subtle shocks Hitchcock ever devised. Nothing was prepared, as in a thriller. One moment the wife, though obviously very worried, was behaving normally and the next—as we slowly began to notice in the course of a quiet scene with a lawyer—her face had become quite blank, the eyes dead, the will-power completely eroded.

Individuals under such pressure were disquieting to contemplate. In everyday life, the general tendency would be to regard them as misfits. For reasons they couldn't help, they were maladjusted. Yet, society at large was responsible: these individuals were human, and their problems belonged to humanity.

The misfit who seeks a fresh lease on life was represented by Private O'Meara (Rod Steiger) in Samuel Fuller's *Run of the Arrow* (1956). Although it was set in the 1860s, the film related quite readily to the social climate of the Fifties. O'Meara was a Virginian, filled with hatred for the conquering Northerners and determined to continue his opposition to them when the Civil War had ended. For this reason he joined the Sioûx Indians, qualifying for the privilege by submitting to one of their ritual trials of strength: running for survival, pursued by warriors who fired arrows at him as he ran. Having survived, he was accepted

*Rod Steiger (right) as the Virginian who became a
member of the Sioux in RUN OF THE ARROW*

by the tribe; but he discovered in the course of time that for him, as
for many others in any era, a retreat from one society into another was
not feasible.

The desire for a new orientation was a problem examined repeatedly
in Hollywood movies of the Fifties. Contemporary bids for escape, or
alienation, were epitomised in addiction to drugs. Otto Preminger's *The
Man with the Golden Arm* (1955), from the novel by Nelson Algren,
was objective in its study of the addict's compulsion, and Frank Sinatra's performance as the poker-dealer, whose "golden arm" became an
ironic metaphor, was a valuable aid to understanding. So was Don
Murray, in *A Hatful of Rain* (1957), from the play by Michael Vincente Grazzo. The machine-tooled craftsmanship of the plot was probably more effective in the theatre, but Fred Zinnemann's direction of
the movie was assured. Withdrawal agonies, from heroin in the first
movie and morphine in the second, were convincingly portrayed; and

Don Murray as a morphine addict and Eva Marie Saint as his wife in A HATFUL OF RAIN

the reliance upon drug pedlars was emphasised, making it clear that a better remedy was needed than the useless measure of placing the addicts themselves outside the law.

Reliance upon drugs could be traced to any number of causes, among them the sad overlap from the original use of a drug for medical reasons. The tendency, in conjunction with the suicidal urge as depicted in *Fourteen Hours* and the escapist drive epitomised in *Run of the Arrow,* signified that it was indeed time to question the structures of society. Over the years, a malaise had taken hold upon many individuals.

So it was appropriate in 1950 for George Stevens to make a new film version of Theodore Dreiser's novel *An American Tragedy,* now called *A Place in the Sun*: a steady and derisive gaze at the U.S.A.'s departure from the Lincoln principle that "all men are created equal."

The story had been filmed before in 1931 by Josef von Sternberg. Its critical attitude remained valid across the decade: the malaise of society was not a new thing, but it had increased to disturbing proportions. The Stevens film had a certain pictorial gloss, a *prolongement* of the Hollywood sheen, eloquently black-and-white, a carry-over from the style of the Forties, marking clear distinctions between gracious living and shadowy poverty; with Montgomery Clift as the sensitive and hapless victim of his conformist background, Elizabeth Taylor as the girl who was part of it, and Shelley Winters as the factory worker, underprivileged and pregnant, whose equivocal death on Loon Lake brought the man to trial for her murder. The social demarcations remained highly relevant. Many divisions existed within the U.S.A.'s wishful framework of democracy.

Joanne Woodward and Patricia Owens as inhabitants of a compact housing estate where individuality is frustrated, in NO DOWN PAYMENT

Glossier, and hardly in the Dreiser class but nevertheless quite pertinent to the social *mores* of the U.S.A., was the composite picture of life in a small New England township, culled (and partially cleansed) from the long Grace Metalious novel *Peyton Place* (1957, Mark Robson). It was an intermittently ludicrous film, primarily because the condensation of plot made one calamity follow upon another in such rapid succession: a girl's hysterical reaction to the news that she was illegitimate was topped immediately by the discovery of a dead body hanging in her wardrobe, for example. Yet, in many a small town where community existence is tight and tense, nervous excesses are frequent. The festering incidents of *Peyton Place* included lust in the shack of an impoverished drunkard who raped his step-daughter, a murder trial in which Lana Turner strayed wildly from the point as she gave her evidence (very realistic touch, in fact), and the multiplicity of gossip from mean minds, devoid of occupation, spreading harm in a milieu where the keeping up of appearances was regarded more favourably than spiritual freedom. Human nature was compared, unfavourably, to the beauty of nature: the woods beyond the town were russet and warm. On Sundays, the self-righteous divided themselves into groups at their various churches, less to worship than to show their devotion on their sleeves, where the neighbours could take note of it.

Life was a mess in *Peyton Place,* but the town looked neat, as did the geometrical segments of a Californian housing estate in *No Down Payment* (1957, Martin Ritt), from the novel by John McPartland: a topical indictment of the new suburbia, constructed with every technological asset, spacially economic, making a bid for gracious neighbourly living by juxtaposing four backyards that were conducive to alfresco barbecue parties—and also to house-to-house darting by any husband who happened to covet his neighbour's wife. Four married couples ran the soap-opera gambit, from dewy-eyed romance that was doomed to disenchantment, to the liquor-drench of misery for a neglected girl (Joanne Woodward) whose spouse (Cameron Mitchell) had enjoyed the recent war and developed from it a sinister urge to become a policeman and be legally violent: his sadistic lust was eliminated, along with his wretched life, when his wife gave him a bad-tempered push while he was changing a car wheel, and the full weight of the status-vehicle came down on top of him. The *genre,* in respect of characters and incidents, was common; but the setting gave a special edge to *No Down*

Payment. Development estates, where conformity was purchased on the installment plan, were represented as a threat to peaceable co-existence. The families were too close together. Individuality was not taken into account. Anyone who did not conform was automatically a misfit.

During the Fifties, the conformist state of mind in the U.S.A. grew stronger—a bulwark against the threat of Communism. Individual thinkers were disturbed; and their disturbance was reflected effectively in movies like *Peyton Place* and *No Down Payment.* Beneath the surface gloss, and despite the tailored plots, these films were astringent: far removed from those artificial happy families of the Hollywood past. The parent-and-child relationship, venerated during the Forties in "man-to-man" conversations between ancient Judge Hardy (Lewis Stone) and his scatterbrained offspring Andy (Mickey Rooney—invariably looking young enough to be the old goat's grandson), gave place by 1954 to the forthrightness of *Rebel without a Cause.* This realistic variation upon the timeless theme of the generation gap was beautifully directed by Nicholas Ray, with James Dean as the rootless boy at a high school where a fellow-student gashed the tyre of his car and provoked him to a knife-fight, leading on to "the chicken run"—a demonstration of bravado by two opponents, each in a separate car, driving fast over ground which terminated at a high clifftop where the cars would go on to oblivion but the first boy to jump clear would be "chicken." Dean made the chicken-jump, while his opponent "won"—and died. The incident, filmed with tremendous tension, triggered the conflict at the heart of the movie: the communication barrier between Dean and his parents. Their marriage was maladjusted, the wife continually brow-beating the husband, but what they had in common was a fear of notoriety which might set them apart from conformist society. This was the consideration uppermost in their minds when Dean told them about the accident, and of his own resolve to go to the police. They opposed the idea, preferring to hush up any scandal. The situation brought into the open a deep antagonism between father and son in a scene powerfully acted by Dean and Jim Backus.

The theme persisted in the years immediately following. It prefigured the breakaway of young people in the Sixties, the hippies and the drop-outs—the protesters, violent or non-violent according to individual proclivities, typifying a concerted discontent with the accepted values of family life, and of society at large. A step ahead of the cinema, of

Variegated idols of the Fifties. Above: Elvis Presley (left); James Dean (right, with Sal Mineo) in REBEL WITHOUT A CAUSE. Below: Mario Lanza

course, were such fine and influential novelists as J. D. Salinger, author of *The Catcher in the Rye,* whose writing expressed the adolescent postwar irritation, and Jack Kerouac who spoke for the Beat generation of the Fifties.

It was a long term problem, bruited spasmodically in Hollywood films of previous decades, usually with an upbeat resolution that rang untrue. *Rebel without a Cause,* if only because of its commercial success, sparked off the usual string of imitative films, ranging from the meretricious to the admirable. *The Blackboard Jungle* (1955, Richard Brooks), from a widely read novel by Evan Hunter, would doubtless have been made without any other spur than the book's accepted value. It depicted a school of overcrowded classrooms, where the pupils came from less affluent families and were given to ganging up upon their teachers; one boy was on the point of raping a female member of the staff in an unfrequented part of the building, when the leading character, an understanding but tough male teacher (Glenn Ford) intervened and was subsequently beaten in a side street by a bunch of his hoodlum students. In the wider world beyond the schoolrooms, crime was rife among the young: perhaps Hollywood exaggerated this by the very quantity of movies that had sensational appeal, combining violence with social concern in proportions that were often dubiously balanced. Yet, even among the low budget films, one found the odd work of art. Irvin Kershner's *Stakeout on Dope Street* (1958) was unexpectedly graphic and credible in its moody observation of three young adults of humble stock who happened to find a container full of heroin, abandoned in a hurry by some criminals who wanted it back. Melodrama arose from the threat to the boys, from criminals and police alike, while moral issues were given their due weight at the same time. One of the boys favoured the responsible civic attitude of going at once to the police and handing over the heroin, but he was repeatedly persuaded by the strongest of the three to see the financial benefits they could gain if they sold their bounty in small portions to a pedlar, who was given a share of the running time to evoke the suffering and degradation of his clients in grim flashbacks. Here, the balance of commerce and conscience was so neat that one might have been regaled with just another second feature, among many, which rode a fashionably downbeat bandwagon. *Stakeout on Dope Street* was exceptional. Its realistic black-and-white photography explored sleazy locations around Los

111

Angeles, and dwelt in grey persuasion upon the three boys in their shabby meeting place behind a grocery shop, considering in their half-formulated minds the possibilities of illicit grandeur, punitive retribution, or simply acceptance of their unpromising status in life. The young actors, Jonathon Haze, Yale Wexler and Morris Miller did not become Hollywood names as a result; nor did Irvin Kershner have the opportunities to follow up this notable cinema *début* as handsomely as some of the other directors who, like himself, had emerged from TV.

Established Hollywood directors were as quick as the new men to latch on to a good money-spinning theme at the behest of astute producers. The plight of youth took on a kind of glamour: a phenomenon stretched to its ultimate extreme when the rock 'n' roll star of the day, Elvis Presley, was directed by Richard Thorpe in *Jailhouse Rock* (1957). Presley, in his early twenties, was doing for 'teenagers of the Fifties what Frank Sinatra had done for their parents—only more so. To his vocal style, Presley added a choreographic convulsion which was remarkably flexible in the hip region, punctuating the music with pelvic thrusts of a nature more explicit than was usual in modern dance of the Martha Graham school, let alone in the gathering places of wide-eyed youth. This being so, and much noted in the cinema and elsewhere, it came as a shock of another kind to see him with his thick black hair shorn away to a jailbird crop, representing a child of misfortune who, before he lost his hair, was nearly seduced by a dame in a bar. Her man showed up and turned nasty, whereupon the boy gallantly defended the woman, dealing her lover a blow that killed him. Unintentionally, of course. Then a manslaughter rap, the traumatic haircut, the inevitable riot in the prison dining hall without which no big-house movie was ever quite complete, and the astounding spectacle of Presley stripped to the waist for a lashing by the guards. He redeemed himself and became a non-criminal success as a result of singing and guitar practice in his cell, encouraged by fellow inmates who rattled their appreciation by clanging mugs against the iron bars. Guy Trosper's screenplay was not without humour: at this point, Presley's cellmate remarked, "They're what you might call a captive audience." Nor was it lacking in a touch of controversy: when an investigating committee of senators visited the prison, the warden suggested that it would be a good idea to put on a show, as "a smokescreen." The show, which was televised, gave Presley another reason to sing, advanced the plot, and at the same time implied that prison conditions were not as good as they might be since the "smokescreen" was to the warden's advantage. This point, however, was only a by-the-way thing, as mild as the riot and the flogging by comparison with prison movies of the Thirties, which had their stronger progression in Don Siegel's *Riot in Cell Block 11* (1953). Prison reform has been a continuing subject of importance in the U.S.A., and indeed many other countries; and the Siegel film was memorable not only for its tremendous climactic action but also for the telling glints of individuals in the throng, faces marked with bitterness, carrying imputations greater than the immediate protest over food and cramped quarters, and implicitly questioning the validity of punitive treatment as a cure for crime. *Jailhouse Rock* reduced such matters to the glossy happily-ending status of mass entertainment. Any incidental preaching it had to do in respect of wayward youth would have fallen lightly upon the largely youthful public at which it aimed.

There was perhaps a little irony in the fact that, when he directed it, Richard Thorpe was already in his sixties. Very much the Hollywood all-rounder, he had been equally smooth about drawing the middle-aged and middle-browed segments of society to *The Great Caruso* (1951), a rather awful movie which established an ardent following for the tenor Mario Lanza who was fairly new to cinema, and who continued for a while to demonstrate that the better-known operatic aria, if placed strategically within a soppy format, would draw a crowd as readily as would the rock 'n' roll boys. Thorpe was an efficient professional: all the same to him, one imagined, if the tiny hand were frozen romantically or the pelvis shaken to primitive rhythm—"rock" being a rather polite substitute for another well-known four-letter word. Indeed, the association of "rock" with raunchy youth was established by Hollywood when the unequivocal lyrics of "Rock around the Clock" accompanied the credit titles of *The Blackboard Jungle*.

There was an especially true feeling to the problem of the sixteen-year-old boy who became *The Young Stranger* to his parents, a well-to-do and thoroughly bewildered couple, the father actually "a motion picture executive." This film, in 1957 at the height of the problem-teens vogue, sounded a quiet note of contrast. In part, its genuine quality might be put down to the fact that both the director, John Frankenheimer, and the writer, Robert Dozier, were in their mid-twenties—that much nearer to the age of their central character, who was played by James MacArthur (about twenty himself at the time, but looking younger). Dozier was said to have based the story on an incident in his own life. What made it especially distinctive amid the general sensationalism was the triviality of the boy's misdemeanour: a minor bit of roughhouse in a neighbourhood cinema. The parents, all too ready to heed the sensation-mongers of the period, construed this as the first terrifying symptom of juvenile delinquency. The father, in his influential position, persuaded the cinema manager to drop the charge against his son, but the family relationships were strained considerably. The difference between *The Young Stranger,* which attained a happy ending plausibly, and the general run of delinquent-problem movies was its moderation. Ironically, too, it was one of Hollywood's takeovers from TV, in which medium it had been directed initially by Frankenheimer, who went on to make a notable cinema career for himself in the Sixties.

Another fine director from TV who maintained a place in cinema was Robert Mulligan. In the same year as Frankenheimer's *The Young Stranger,* Mulligan applied the forthright and full-blooded tactics which were needed for a more extreme, but equally truthful case of the father-and-son dilemma, *Fear Strikes Out* (1957). Here we had the antithesis of delinquency. The story came from the autobiography of a baseball player, Jim Piersall of the Boston Red Sox. It recounted the deplorable and timeless agony of a son who is not merely exhorted, but driven beyond the limits of reason, by a father's ambitions for him. This was depicted as a love-hate relationship, in which the hate was so muted as to be unrecognisable to either the father or the son. Dad (Karl Malden), who was crazy about baseball yet could never make the major league himself, was determined that his son would succeed where he had failed. Jim (Anthony Perkins, superbly right in his interpretation) was over-anxious to please, exhausting himself physically and mentally in his eagerness to comply with his father's wishes. His panic on the field during an important game made a vivid sequence. Even more potent, however, familiar as audiences were by then with the methods of psychiatrists, was the moment of truth in a doctor's words and their antagonising effect upon Jim. Unwilling to attribute his own failure, and his term in hospital, to the father he worshipped and dreaded, he shouted in protest: "If it hadn't been for him . . . I wouldn't be where I am today." The line had to be followed, necessarily,

114

The antithesis of delinquency—Anthony Perkins (centre) as Jim Piersall in FEAR STRIKES OUT

by the serious counterpart of that old comic standby, the double take. Perkins brought it off magnificently; and in no uncertain terms, Mulligan had created the hypertense dramatic atmosphere to sustain it.

The sensitivity of Jim Piersall, expressed in strong terms, might have become old-fashioned had a lesser director been in control. The best movies of these later years of the decade were "cool," as the saying went. And among the very coolest was a portrayal of a singularly insensitive young man, the fictitious but all too credible Claude (Vince Edwards) in *Murder by Contract* (1958), directed by Irving Lerner, who was best known for his work on short films (especially the witty and mildly lyrical *Muscle Beach* of 1948). A second feature running only eighty minutes, *Murder by Contract* was made in haste on a very low budget and turned out to be brilliant. Crisply written by Ben Simcoe, it stated the individual character of Claude in economic terms:

here we saw the man whose ethos is totally amoral, the mercenary killer, available for hire. His assignment was to kill a woman who was due to give evidence in a trial: evidence that Claude's immediate employers wanted to silence. Claude's initial failures discouraged those who had hired him, so they decided to have him killed as a safety measure and take other steps to eradicate the woman. Claude offset this by killing the men who came to murder him, and continued to attempt to fulfil his contract until the police brought him down in a rain of gunfire. Elementary thick-ear melodrama, one might have supposed: but no, it was an astringently cold look at the nature of a cold-blooded young criminal; cinematically efficient, psychologically sound.

6. Acting and Being

FOR ONE OF THE OUTDOOR SHOTS in *Baby Doll* (1956), Carroll Baker, who played the title role, had to cry. The way she did so was considered inadequate during rehearsals, by the actress herself and also in the opinion of the director Elia Kazan, who hit upon a remedy. "I'd worked for several hours and I had gotten desperate," said Kazan, "because a film director always keeps his eye on the sun. Every few minutes or so he looks up at the sun to see how it's doing up there, whether clouds are coming to cover it, or whether it's getting too low so that the light will go soon. And when it began to go down and this girl wasn't able to do the scene right, I was just on the verge of giving it up when I thought of one last desperate effort to jog her into something. Furthermore she wanted to be jogged. She was practically begging me to be mean to her, she was so disgusted with herself and so anxious to do it right. She's a very good actress, incidentally. So I said to her, 'Look—I just don't think you're *able* to do it.' And she burst into tears and never stopped. From then on, I got all the takes I needed." In the completed film, it looked real: to a certain degree, it *was* real. Yet, in Kazan's view, it was also good acting: "Of course it's acting. It's part of the performance. Stage actors do similar things at times. They have to find some way. There's nothing worse than a stage actor faking emotion. An audience is too aware of real emotion now, too sophisticated to be fooled very often."

Carroll Baker's instinctive response was not gained by the bullying of a martinet, but more probably because the actress felt that Kazan had lost confidence in her. His remark to her was a white lie, spoken quietly no doubt. When Patricia Neal was directed by Kazan in *A Face in the Crowd* (1957), she was impressed by the calm that seemed to emanate from him, something described by Kazan himself as "a technique," aligned with tenacity: "I've been around long enough to know that if you don't get it right the first time, you can try again. And I do. I just persist. The point of the calm that I try to get on a set is that it reassures actors. It makes them feel safe. It makes them feel relaxed, too. They feel that there isn't anyone frantically worried and

Karl Malden and Carroll Baker in BABY DOLL—"Of course it's acting," said Kazan

waiting for them to perform, but there's someone who has confidence in them, who can control the vast mechanism so that it's there to serve them, and not vice versa. Someone who is there to help them, and believes in them. Actors need it. They're like children. They need the sense of a roof over their head and a confident father who is all for them."

Kazan's extreme measure of seemingly withdrawing his confidence from Carroll Baker (for which she expressed both approval and gratitude subsequently) had an outcome which erased the dividing line that can separate "acting" from "being." In the Fifties, such erasions were frequent. Previously, Hollywood had preserved a measure of formalism, partly a hangover from the silent days when gesture was a substitute for speech and Griffith told Lillian Gish to observe the movements of both humans and animals, and to adapt them for her own refinements of mime. With the arrival of sound, when certain silent actors proved quite capable of using their vocal chords, there was a period of stagey transition in film acting, protracted by the importation of theatre performers who had been conditioned to project across footlights. For example, the hyper-expressive faces and gesticulative hands of Norma Shearer and Jeanette MacDonald during the Thirties could be attributed to their respective assimilations of techniques related to the silent cinema and the opera house. Very gradually, such things were moderated. By the Fifties it was recognised that film acting could be more instinctive. Since a poor take had always been expendable, finance and weather permitting, many directors encouraged their players to "let themselves go" on the understanding that if they went too far there would still be a chance to improve. In Robert Aldrich's *Attack!* (1956), Eddie Albert played an army captain who lost his nerve and became hysterical under pressure of wartime duties: a remarkable extension of range for Albert, established in amiable roles during the Thirties and Forties. Aldrich directed him in accordance with the theory that "with proper rehearsal you build up to a point where an actor emotionally identifies with a part and gets better and better. You smooth out all the mechanics, the props and the camera movements and everything else, so that at the point when the actor really starts to function it can be captured on the film and held. For Eddie's big breakdown scene, all this had been properly prepared and all adequate rehearsals had been done and Eddie was starting to function very well. On the take he was proceeding magnificently and the anticipated climax would have come at the right time. His complete disintegration as a person . . . as an actor. But Eddie thought that he was progressing too quickly, that he would reach the climax too soon, and his fear of not being able to sustain the crisis long enough made him stop and cut the take himself. Now this is a tragedy. So, you know . . . you just walk the other way and come back and say 'Do it again.' But you *know* that kind of emotional identification will never be captured again. It will be good, it may even be exciting, but you just can't recapture that original degree of impact." The take Aldrich used was indeed exciting: so much so as to make one think that Eddie Albert's spontaneous decision might have been for the best. The director observes, and knows what he wants. The actor's emotion here was not divorced from a cerebral attitude towards what he was doing.

When Aldrich spoke of his "disintegration as a person . . as an actor" the fusion of character and performer was implicit. The Fifties saw an important development in screen acting. It was not without precedent. It was a progression from the mime of Lillian Gish, who certainly identified with the characters she played. More emphatically, it derived from a precept of Constantin Stanislavsky, a founder of the Moscow Art Theatre, whose book *An Actor Prepares* contains the vital injunction: "You must live the part every moment you are playing it." For half a century, Stanislavsky's theories were known to many actors and teachers. Michael Chekhov, who had worked with him in Russia, went to Hollywood in the Forties, where he acted in movies (among them Hitchcock's *Spellbound*) and imparted much knowledge to his students there. But the name of Stanislavsky impinged freshly, and in some cases too astringently for comfort, upon the cracked ivory tower of American cinema in 1950, the year Marlon Brando came west. Born in Omaha, Brando spent his early life there and in Illinois before he moved to New York at the age of nineteen and began taking lessons in acting. His drama coach was Stella Adler. Broadway audiences saw him first as a juvenile in John van Druten's *I Remember Mama*; by 1946 he was playing Marchbanks opposite Katherine Cornell in Shaw's *Candida*; and the following year he appeared as Stanley Kowalski opposite Jessica Tandy as Blanche Dubois in *A Streetcar Named Desire* by Tennessee Williams. This play was the making of him. His performance drew the town, praise for it echoed around the world, and

Hollywood took notice. As a corollary, word also spread that the secret of Brando's success was due in no small measure to improvisational sessions at The Actors Studio in New York, where Lee Strasberg and Elia Kazan and others had begun during the Forties to hold classes for performers who wished to flex their talents. The ethos of The Actors Studio was based upon Stanislavsky principles of concentration, personal involvement through seeking equivalents in one's own experience to create an identification with the character portrayed, either by emotive memory or perceptive observation, and willingness to improvise without inhibitions.

Brando's first movie, *The Men* (1950) was directed by Fred Zinnemann, who felt that "it was difficult for him to make the transition from stage acting to screen acting. When he has troubles he likes to withdraw within himself. It's not easy to reach him. So that, at times, becomes quite a problem. But he struck me as a man of extreme and very exciting talent." Brando was cast as a paraplegic, a victim of war. The performance involved great physical control as the character, deprived of the use of his legs, exercised the muscles of his arms and torso; equally, the screenplay by Carl Foreman delineated the mental stress and self-pity of a virile man reduced to virtually half of his former self. As a test piece in another medium, it was passed quite admirably by Brando, although his full quality was not to be gauged until one recalled the sensitivity of this performance while observing the animal demeanour he adopted in the film version of *A Streetcar Named Desire,* directed by Kazan later in the same year. Vivien Leigh played the neurotic Blanche. Already familiar with the role (in the London stage production she had been directed by Laurence Olivier), she brought a touching vulnerability to the woman's precarious imbalance: like several other women in the *oeuvre* of Tennessee Williams, Blanche tries to maintain a romantic image against which reality grates unkindly—destructively when reality takes the brutish form of Kowalski, applying a coarse humour and a blatant sexuality to his assault upon Blanche's fragile delusions of grace. Their confrontations were memorable. The realism of Brando dominated, possibly because he was new to cinema and highly original, possibly because we knew Vivien Leigh's ability

Opposite: Marlon Brando in (above left) ON THE WATERFRONT, (above right) GUYS AND DOLLS, (below left) A STREETCAR NAMED DESIRE, and (below right) JULIUS CAESAR

and her magnificent performance came as no surprise; or because (but this I doubt) there was a grain of truth in something Tennessee Williams said when I asked him if he found it easier to write the realistic lines of Kowalski or the lyrical words of Blanche: "I'm not quite sure. I think perhaps a hard, realistic kind of dialogue is easier for me. Perhaps I stretch a little for the other. Maybe that's why it isn't as much appreciated." Kazan, on another occasion, said that he had "always thought of the stage as rather more poetic" than cinema, "not that the screen isn't poetic also, but I've always thought the theatre at its best when it was unrealistic." It seems likely, as well, that cinema drew even closer attention than theatre to Brando's ability to identify, to "be" rather than to "act." Kazan, who directed him as Kowalski on Broadway as well as in the movie, believes that "you can photograph thinking —that is, very often in close-up you get so close to an actor that you can see the process of thought, or think you can: actually what you see is some exterior manifestation of what's happening inside, so small that you wouldn't notice it except with the camera very close." It was Kazan again who directed Brando in *Viva Zapata!* (1952), notable for its atmospheric black-and-white cinematography by Joseph MacDonald and its screenplay by John Steinbeck, as well as the superb compositions Kazan devised to bring a considerable visual poetry to groups of Mexicans united by Zapata in revolt against the Diaz regime of 1910; the uses of sound were concomitantly impressive: a clicking of stones in token of protest, a proliferation of gunfire in an overhead shot as the trapped figure of Zapata crumbled under the hail of bullets. Brando's chameleon transformation made Zapata a man of contradictions, and therefore a whole man, a creature of strengths and doubts, humble to the point of self-denigration and yet imbued with the spirit to fight injustice.

Arousing insurgents in more articulate tones, Brando's inner fire never came fully to terms with the metrical demands of Shakespeare's Marc Antony in *Julius Caesar* (1953). A naturalistic film, directed by Joseph L. Mankiewicz, accommodated the realism of Brando well enough, provided one considered the performance as a display of virtuosity, isolating the vow over Caesar's dead body and the political application of psychology in the forum as two remarkable speeches. In workshop sessions at The Actors Studio, Brando had applied his gifts to Shakespeare, and for that matter to Chekhov and Molière as well.

Modulated emotionally to cinema, his Antony spanned the centuries and became meaningful in relationship to Twentieth-century struggles for power. Yet neither of Antony's great set pieces had sufficient respect for the verse; and, while each of them compelled admiration for Brando's empathy, they were embodied in a film that ran a considerable gamut of acting styles, with John Gielgud's eloquent Cassius at one extreme, Brando at the other, and in between them a diversity of talents that could not be fused. James Mason's Brutus was a tidy compromise in the circumstances, occasionally pulling a few strands together, and when he played the famous quarrel scene with Gielgud we had another isolated occasion to remember from a movie lacking the overall unity of acting that such a work demands.

A return to the comparatively inarticulate was Brando's violent delinquent in *The Wild One* (1953), directed by Laslo Benedek with appropriate choreography for motor-cycles. Ridden by a sizeable pack of restive youths, led by a leather-clad Brando, the cycles thrummed towards a retreating camera *en route* to a small and rather mean-minded township, where a frightened girl was ensnared in the slowly gyrating circle of bikes and boys. The gang wrecked the town. The destructive urge, which tends to find such outlets between wars, was noted. But there were those who looked upon it as incitement rather than indictment. In retrospect it seems mild, because life and movies grew wilder over the years. The motor-cycle as a symbol of release, in Dennis Hopper's *Easy Rider* (1969), or of menace, in Roger Corman's *The Wild Angels* (1965), and of course as a symbol of sex for many moons, had not attained its apotheosis with Brando astride it. Nevertheless, in its day, the machine and the leather outfit gave him a certain image in the public eye, which he proceeded to diminish, or at any rate change, with his portrait of Napoleon in *Désirée* (1954, directed by Henry Koster and based on a novel by Annemarie Selinko). The girl of the title, played by Jean Simmons, was a pre-Josephine dalliance; the whole thing looked merely expensive; and for the first time in Brando's film career it seemed that the chameleon's permutations were not infinite. Here was an actor in search of a character, obviously in need of help, especially in the matter of his voice which he was probably trying to adapt to some interior concept but which came out strangely clipped and artificial.

Enthusiasm was soon to be restored. The affirmation of Brando's

unique gift as an actor came in Kazan's *On the Waterfront* (1954).
Beyond this there would be further variations: an entertaining but
scarcely remarkable sketch of a Damon Runyon gambler in the musical
Guys and Dolls (1955, Joseph L. Mankiewicz); a very sprightly Oki-
nawan interpreter, foxing the U.S. occupation into providing an underprivileged village with *The Teahouse of the August Moon* (1956, Daniel Mann); a racially prejudiced American major whose attitude was
changed when he fell in love with a Matsubayashi actress in Japan,
making a commendable point rather cloyingly before they said *Sayo-
nara* (1957); a German officer of the Second World War whose pacifist
inclinations were undermined but not obliterated by notions of duty in
The Young Lions (1958, Edward Dmytryk); and a latterday Orpheus
in a snakeskin jacket, which can be shed with the aid of wishful dreams,
unlike human skin wherein all are imprisoned, whether they settle for
security or emulate the Tennessee Williams nomads epitomised by
Brando in *The Fugitive Kind* (1959, Sidney Lumet). But if any one
film, among these several triumphs and occasional disappointments,
can be singled out as proof that Brando spearheaded a major change
in American cinema acting during the Fifties, that film is surely *On
the Waterfront*.

Corruption festered in the dockers' unions on the New York waterfront, where location filming and Kazan's poetic realism mingled
authentic sounds with unactorish voices as Brando and Eva Marie
Saint walked through grim streets or across a meagre park. The un-
healthy air seemed to assail one's nostrils. The gangdom rule of the
ironically named Friendly (Lee J. Cobb) brought death to anyone who
signified an individual will to resist. Forces of law and religion alike
were powerless, and the ideals of solidarity among workers had been
exploited with a cynicism and ruthlessness that assumed the significance
of a metaphor. Beyond its immediate subject, disturbing in itself and
the prime example of sociological comment rising above the confines
of expedient political pigeon-holes, *On the Waterfront* crystallised the
strongest theme to emerge in American films of its troubled decade: the
rights of the individual, his human entitlement to eschew conformity,
and his suffering in the process. Carried to the symbolic level by several
important writers, in this case Budd Schulberg, the point was brought
home to realists by the simplistic case of Terry Malloy (Brando), a
docker who had done some boxing in his time and was not the brightest

brain on the waterfront, yet had the instinct to distinguish wrong from right. Easily led, he had permitted himself to be a pawn in lethal games on behalf of Friendly. His one-man rebellion at the climax was incited by personal relationships: a forlorn kind of love for the girl whose rebel brother was murdered by Friendly's thugs, with a certain amount of complicity from Terry himself; and a primal urge to avenge the killing of his brother Charley, formerly a legal aide to Friendly and a sharp-witted opportunist, but one who relinquished favour. So Terry Malloy is transmuted from a slow-minded, worried underdog into the solitary redeemer, beaten to a bloody pulp by Friendly's men while his fellow dockers watch and do nothing. His mutilated body can shuffle away through the conformist crowd, a loser of the Twentieth century whose passion burns to the spectator's heart with a purer fire than was ever kindled by Hollywood representations of Calvary.

From the mid-Fifties, through the influence of Kazan, the success of Brando, and the impact of *On the Waterfront,* more and more players from The Actors Studio were drawn to Hollywood. In need of a handy term to classify their philosophy of acting, somebody hit upon "The Method"; and in many mouths it was spoken with contempt. Veterans of the latterday formalism and glamour were sometimes aghast at the new breed. As they grew thicker upon the Californian ground, a quieter dissent was voiced. Calmly but emphatically, Joan Crawford said, "I know there is a new school of acting. We call it the shuffleboard school. It has no effect or bearing on me. I don't believe you want to go to the theatre to see somebody you can see next door. You don't pay for that kind of entertainment; just knock on the door and meet your neighbours." The attitude was prevalent, and there was still a public for Joan Crawford movies. In fact she was doing nicely right throughout the decade, particularly in *Sudden Fear* (1952, David Miller), a nimble and glossy thriller with Jack Palance on hand to frighten her. Palance had understudied Brando, and eventually taken over the role of Kowalski in the Broadway production of *A Streetcar Named Desire.* An actor with the face of a pugilist and the mind of a poet, he seemed to strike appropriate sparks from Joan Crawford. Her persona had graduated gently since her *début* in the Twenties and, fording the decades serenely, her professionalism endured. If representational was the word for her kind of acting, there was still a market for what she represented, which wasn't a mirror held up to the folks next door but a dreamy ideal of the woman whose lipstick was unlikely to smear as her resistance weakened beneath the hot kiss of a hustler (Jeff Chandler) prepared to sell his body to any affluent *Female on the Beach* (1955, Joseph Pevney). Rising to every occasion, she could be tough as a leader of the lawless, even to the climactic shooting of a formidable antagonist (Mercedes McCambridge) in that rummest of Westerns *Johnny Guitar* (1953, Nicholas Ray), or vulnerable yet valiant as a comparatively ordinary and yet most orderly wallflower, taking a husband (Cliff Robertson) younger than herself and nurturing him through a mental breakdown to the lush accompaniment of a soap-operatic title-tune, *Autumn Leaves* (1956, Robert Aldrich). Joan Crawford was not the only manifestation of a glamour that refused to be bygone. In the Fifties, she was the best of her venerable breed.

One must remember, too, a persistent throwback appeal in re-makes of movies that had brought lumps to throats of yore. Jane Wyman bore her share of brunts: as the long-suffering and insufferable mother of *So Big* (1953, Robert Wise) she plucked heartstrings as susceptible as those that Barbara Stanwyck twanged in the same role more than twenty years before; and after a similar time span, she tackled Irene Dunne's old chore in *Magnificent Obsession* (1954, Douglas Sirk) as the bravest of accidentally blinded heroines, with make-up applied so impeccably that she might have been presumed to receive supernatural relief every hour or so to fix up her face at the mirror, and with lines quite rich in their improbability: "Forgive me, I didn't mean to parade my emotions" . . . "I always danced with my eyes closed, anyway." It is the *genre* one derides, not the actress: she was superb as a Tennessee Williams loser, the crippled girl whose reality was despair and whose dreams were restricted to contemplating the fragments of beauty she had collected together and called *The Glass Menagerie* (1950, Irving Rapper).

Another significant throwback was *The Spoilers,* the adventure yarn celebrated for its climax-fight between two men. The apotheosis of cinematic violence, this one began in the silent era and was re-made once in every decade since, from the 1910s to the Fifties when it ran itself as far into the ground as possible with Jeff Chandler and Rory Calhoun swapping the punches (1956, Jesse Hibbs). Affiliated to the medium's potential for realism, to the catharsis of Greek tragedy, and to the glowing moral of good conquering evil, its echoes often reverberated with jocularity through the Westerns of John Ford. There was a significant moral difference between the vicarious, and possibly therapeutic, violence of *The Spoilers* and the beating-up of Terry Malloy in *On the Waterfront* which made a contemporary social comment and led through suffering to a spiritual regeneration. It could be argued, strongly, that an equivalent social value, together with the realism of "photographed thought" and character identification, came across in Gary Cooper's acting for *High Noon* (1952, Fred Zinnemann). And Cooper's acquaintance with the camera had begun in the Twenties: "Doing stunts and falls in cowboy pictures. I never did consider myself much of an actor. There was a big thrill in doing that sort of thing, and stunts paid pretty good money for a small amount of knowledge about how to hit the ground rolling, and not get yourself in a hospital. In lieu of theatrical schooling, I was kept very busy and was fortunate in that I worked with some of the greatest directors and most famous actors." When the talkies began, Cooper's indigenous film acting was not overpowered by talent recruited from the stage. In the early Thirties he played top roles with Charles Laughton and Tallulah Bankhead in *The Devil and the Deep,* with Helen Hayes in *A Farewell to Arms*; he even took a commendable tilt at the sophisticated repartee of Noël Coward's *Design for Living* in company with Miriam Hopkins and Fredric March. Taught by experience, Cooper reflected at the end of the Fifties that "the acting itself, I found, was not as easy as it looked at first. I don't want to sound self-satisfied about the acting thing, because you can do something and maybe some people think it's fine, but you know inside yourself that it can be done better. Even after more than thirty years I feel there's so much to learn. I see young people coming up with various talents. You realise that everyone has many and different things to contribute. So we can never be self-satisfied in our business. And I doubt if any of us really is."

Those last two sentences might have been spoken by a dedicated member of The Actors Studio. Steadily their talents, various indeed, brought a new awareness to Hollywood. Some were called stars: all were deemed actors. Their numbers included Rod Steiger, Ben Gazzara, Paul Newman, Carroll Baker, Eva Marie Saint, Anthony Franciosa, Eli Wallach, Lee J. Cobb, Kim Stanley, Tom Ewell, George Peppard, Arthur Kennedy.

Julie Harris, identifying with the characters she played, contributed strongly to Hollywood's new awareness

Three more in Kazan's *East of Eden* (1954) were Julie Harris, James Dean and Jo Van Fleet. Adapted from a novel by John Steinbeck, the story bore a faint allegorical resemblance to the agony of Cain, as its title implied, and Dean brought to the key role a haunting sorrow. Unnoticed in his previous minor forays into cinema, this actor had attracted some attention on the New York stage in small but effective roles in *See the Jaguar* by N. Richard Nash (author of *The Rainmaker*) and *The Immoralist* by André Gide. Julie Harris was established on Broadway as the twelve-year-old Frankie, a tormented girl shouldering her way desperately towards womanhood in *The Member of the Wedding* by Carson McCullers: showy, of course, because the slightly-built but intense young actress was playing a character half her own age, and she repeated the feat endearingly in a film version directed by Fred Zinnemann in 1952, before returning to New York for the highly contrasted role of Sally Bowles, a sophisticated whirl of free love and prairie oysters, in John Van Druten's comedy from the Christopher Isherwood novel *I Am a Camera*. In both characters, different as they were, bravado concealed insecurity. The actress disclosed this fundamental fear while at the same time combining a wonderful surface comedy with evocations of age and environment: Frankie the adolescent, a product of the Deep South where universal problems are writ large, and Sally the defiantly worldly young woman in the cosmopolitan Berlin that would collapse beneath the conformist heels of the Nazis. The Julie Harris panache as Sally Bowles was to be filmed subsequently in Britain (1955, Henry Cornelius). Her assignment in *East of Eden*, as the conventional and gentle Abra whose passion responded, against her conditioned idea of propriety, to the ardour of the confused and rebellious Cal (Dean), was something more delicate. Without benefit of any big effects, and in company with players who were provided with more outwardly evident advantages in their roles, she maintained an inner warmth and compassion: an identity. Here, indeed, was another chameleon. And the same could be said of Jo Van Fleet, as the mother of Cal, long since departed from home to become the madam of a brothel not too far away for her troubled son to find her. Already versatile on the stage, the measure of her talent would become even clearer in other films: as Doc Holliday's woman in *Gunfight at the OK Corral* (1957, John Sturges) and more especially as the stubborn old defender of property against governmental pressure in the cause of development and progress in *Wild River* (1959, Kazan).

Whether James Dean was quite such a chameleon has remained in doubt. He died in a car accident, in October of 1955, at the age of twenty-four. Consequently his popularity was mainly posthumous, even verging upon necrophilia in extreme instances of youthful filmgoers who saw in his performances a close affinity with their own resentment of parental disciplines. This image of Dean as the archetypal victim of an unbridgeable generation gap had begun with *East of Eden*. He was so right and true as Cal that spectators accustomed to accepting the actor as the character were instinctive in their response. In fact, there can be little doubt that what they saw in him on the screen was an inherited wishfulness of their own. The parents from whom they felt so hopelessly removed in attitude had identified equally in previous years with star images who stood for the kind of lives they would like to lead, the kind of glamour they coveted for themselves. Dean brought it closer, because he acted better. And Cal was undoubtedly a magnificent example of the individual at loggerheads with a hidebound father and with people of his own age who belonged to a community in which ideas and codes were inflexible. It made little difference that the period was before and during the First World War. The obsessions carried across the decades, just as their origins were to be found in the scriptures. Cal's father was called Adam (Raymond Massey), and he was a tight-minded bigot, humiliated by his wife's departure and seeing in Cal an irritating reminder of her personality. Therefore Adam's favourite was his other son Aron (Richard Davalos), an upright boy, not to say self-righteous. Yet he was not to be dismissed lightly. When the war had broken out and the townsfolk attack a German shoemaker who has been living and working in their midst, Aron is the first to protest. Then Cal supports his brother, hot-blood personified, fists ready for practical action, starting up a minor battle which ruins the German's garden. Aron, a thoroughgoing pacifist, rebukes Cal, who retaliates in the manner of Cain: he doesn't kill his brother, but does give him a sound beating. Aron's betrothal to Abra is a further demeanment for Cal; and an even more hurtful setback is Adam's refusal of money offered him by Cal in an effort to gain parental affection. Adam's own business plans have gone awry, leaving him financially in need, but he construes as profiteering Cal's industrious efforts to cultivate beans and sell them during the wartime food shortage. Everything the boy attempts would seem to confirm his outlaw status. Indeed, the upbeat ending, a reconciliation between Adam and Cal arranged through the good-hearted intervention of Abra, would scarcely have been plausible but for the inner grace of Julie Harris as this girl whose meekness cloaks the moral strength to make an old man see the injustice of his ways.

Cal, in elation when his crops are doing well, in compulsive violence and love-making, in resentment and even in spite, was a forerunner of the modern misfit of *Rebel without a Cause* (1954), whose conflict with his parents served to emphasise the identification point for youth of the Fifties. A social demarcation between his middle-class rebel and the arrogant hoodlum played by Brando in *The Wild One* was not

Opposite: Julie Harris—with Ethel Waters and Brandon de Wilde (above) in THE MEMBER OF THE WEDDING; with Richard Davalos and James Dean (below) in EAST OF EDEN

sufficient in itself to obliterate the similarity between Dean and Brando. Unalike in appearance, they nevertheless had much the same mode of speech, and to a certain degree the same manner of deportment, befitting the characters they played. Like the Brando of *A Streetcar Named Desire* and *The Wild One,* Dean in both *East of Eden* and *Rebel without a Cause* was inclined to mumble his lines, as such characters would, and as a result the conventional minds who regarded clarity of speech as a prerequisite for any actor in any role were quick to deride the two of them. To be sure, it wasn't always easy to understand what they said; and this was realism. More importantly, it was impossible to misinterpret what they were thinking and feeling, not as actors but as characters within the circumstances of the given films; and this was realism, too, of a kind more potent than could ever be conveyed merely through words, however clearly and passionately enunciated. In the mind of Julie Harris there was no question of limitation in Dean's work: "Jimmy had the temperament of a really versatile actor. I think, if he'd lived, he'd have been one of the finest."

Dean's third and last film, *Giant* (1955, George Stevens), went a long way towards substantiating this opinion. Again the slur and the slouch and the defiance; but, more than this, a progression from bitter youth to hardened maturity. The story was derived from an Edna Ferber novel which fanned considerable resentment in Texas, the giant state of the title, denigrated as a vast breeding-ground for the materialist ethos. Dean played Jett Rink, a ranch hand too arrogant to be an underdog, imparting through his eyes rather than his speech a declaration of love for his employer's wife (Elizabeth Taylor), eventually making his fortune in oil and then, at the age of fifty, wooing her nubile daughter (Carroll Baker) in the deserted bar of his own luxury hotel, inebriated, semi-articulate, true—never truer to character than when, increasingly drunk, he bespeaks the racial prejudice in his blood by scorning the same girl's Mexican sister-in-law. This should have been enough to sunder that dubious identification between enlightened youth and the living image of a dead man up there on the screen. But perhaps the image established in the previous two films was the one they chose to remember. Jett was hardly a sympathetic guy, but he was the most real, and perhaps the most understandable, of Dean's three magnificent portraits.

Both Dean and Brando were seemingly imitated by a small rash of young actors in the mid-Fifties, especially when Hollywood embarked upon one of its commercial cycles, making a number of films about juvenile delinquency (some quite good) to cash in on the bandwagon that began rolling with *The Wild One* and *Rebel without a Cause*. What might also have been construed as an imitation of Brando occurred, however, in a quasi-epic of rather more than the normal improbability of its kind, *The Silver Chalice* (1954, Victor Saville). The principal character, a silversmith converted to Christianity after many obligatory displays of action and sex had reeled their way through the projectors, marked the initial Hollywood appearance of Paul Newman, fresh from a healthy Broadway season in William Inge's *Picnic*. To the era of Nero, he brought a Brandoesque modernity: he looked a bit like Brando, he talked a bit like Brando. Some years later, when everybody knew he was no copy but a performer of distinct individuality, he was able to be objective and self-critical about this unfortunate start in movies: "It was a terrible mistake. I have no excuses to offer: it was pretty bad." Back on Broadway, he did well again in a thriller by Joseph Hayes, *The Desperate Hours,* although he was not in the subsequent film version directed by William Wyler in 1955. But in 1956 Newman was firmly instated as a cinema actor of consequence, when he gave a brilliant performance as the prizefighter Rocky Graziano in *Somebody Up There Likes Me*. Certainly the prevalent rebel strain of the era was paralleled by the movie's impressions of Graziano's youth in New York slums, where poverty led to petty crime and the aggressive instinct flourished in numerous clashes with a drunken father, juvenile gangs, and the authorities. A readiness with his fists was channelled into a profitable, if unsteady, career as a boxer; and Newman had the physical shape to make this believable. At the same time, his sensitivity and the astute direction of Robert Wise kept the potential aura of a tearjerker well under control. One might detect affinities with Brando still, and with Dean, and for that matter with the Dead End Kids of Hollywood's Thirties, since mutations of put-upon youth fighting back have repeatedly been considered ripe for dramatisation.

For a time, Newman played subtle variations upon the theme, establishing a marked flexibility in the process. *The Long, Hot Summer* (1957, Martin Ritt) took him off at a slight tangent from the increasingly familiar route of the maverick. As Ben Quick, a barn-burner thrown out of one town and determined to make good elsewhere in his own independent fashion, Newman's performance held glints of wry humour and also of mystery, as well as the sexual assurance of an uninhibited male who knew that in this respect at least his life could be as rich as he chose to make it. Selfish and wily, he eased his path to acceptance in an over-heated household, rife with frustrations. Mississippi psychoses were exploited or relieved by his presence. The insecure son of the family could be duped to Ben Quick's financial advantage, while the strong-minded daughter would undoubtedly yield at last to his infallible magnetism. Whether or not he was to be regarded cautiously, as one of nature's barn-burners, remained a little doubtful in spite of the smooth ending to an otherwise trenchant movie, derived from a couple of Deep Southern tales by William Faulkner.

Then in 1958, Newman made two further progressions. As William Bonney in *The Left Handed Gun* he was required to depict the notorious young Western renegade as an underprivileged illiterate, accustomed to lethal violence since childhood, more to be pitied than hero-worshipped. The movie was the best of several attempts to cut the Western myth down to size. For the unsophisticated, who had been inclined to assume that Hollywood's usual evocations of good-and-evil in the open spaces (*circa* 1880) were realistic, here was a plain man's William Bonney, identifiable with the hoodlum of any vintage, and a startling contrast to glamorised interpretations of the same historic figure by Robert Taylor in *Billy the Kid* (1941, David Miller) or Jack Beutel in *The Outlaw* (1940: direction begun by Howard Hawks and completed by the film's producer, Howard Hughes). In retrospect, *The Left Handed Gun* has acquired a higher prestige than it can support, in my view. With a good screenplay by Leslie Stevens, from a play by Gore Vidal, it introduced as a cinema director Arthur Penn, who displayed considerable promise, which he was to fulfil a few years later, notably in *Mickey One* (1965) and *Bonnie and Clyde* (1967). His visual sense was apparent, as indeed was his quest for verisimilitude in the kind of characters so often pigeon-holed as "types," and at a time when colour had become a commercial necessity for the majority of Westerns it was conducive to realism to shoot *The Left Handed Gun* in black-and-white and to drain away the slightest trace of gloss. By comparison, *Cowboy* (1957, Delmer Daves, with Jack Lemmon as a

Opposite: Paul Newman and Elizabeth Taylor in CAT ON A HOT TIN ROOF

young and fairly wide-eyed Frank Harris, flinching from the raw life on the cattle trails) belied its anti-romantic intentions with every Technicolored vista of horsemen and herds in dusty sunlight. But Newman's offbeat and possibly authentic diminishment of the Western hero was a useful step in the right direction as an actor, followed very neatly by a creditable stride into Tennessee Williams territory. In *Cat on a Hot Tin Roof* (1958, Richard Brooks), Newman played Brick, a role created on Broadway by Ben Gazzara. This was a challenge, partly to draw a clean division between his personal style and the Brando heritage, but also to convey the mental distress of a former athlete with an unacknowledged homosexual proclivity and an edgy half-bantering, half-venomous relationship with his bitter yet ultimately compassionate wife (Elizabeth Taylor). Later in the same year, he switched effectively to brisk comedy, together with his wife Joanne Woodward, in *Rally round the Flag, Boys* (1958, Leo McCarey).

Altogether, Newman's films of the Fifties displayed more versatility than Hollywood tended to associate with its imports from The Actors Studio, possibly because he was given better chances than most to ring a few changes. His work at the Studio had begun when he was in New York with *Picnic*. Before then his acting had been, as he put it himself, "academic." In 1959 he was on Broadway again, playing the lead opposite Geraldine Page in Tennessee Williams's *Sweet Bird of Youth,* and being slightly put out at matinees when certain matronly commuters in the front row were given to remarking upon the singular blueness of his eyes in penetrating whispers at the height of a dramatic climax. At such moments, the academician must have come to the aid of the interior stylist which he had tried so diligently, and successfully, to become: "I think The Actors Studio was probably the greatest single contribution to whatever I have today. It exposed me to an entirely different way of thinking. I was very fortunate because I had fourteen months in *Picnic,* during which I had no financial worries and I could devote myself to study. I learned an awful lot by observation of other people in class. It's refreshing and invigorating to find a different kind of expression for yourself. I'm sort of a cerebral actor. Joanne [Woodward] is very different; she's an instinctive emotional actress. I enjoy things cerebrally first, and then see if I can accommodate them emotionally. It's really a tremendous amount of hard work; people who act very instinctively get emotional freedom, and enjoyment, out of propelling themselves into another character. I wish it were easier for me, but it isn't." Setting aside *The Silver Chalice,* no evidence of this problem has been noticeable in any of his films, which seems to indicate that The Actors Studio, for all the tales one heard about physical aids to realism, was essentially concerned with the interior rapport between actor and character.

Julie Harris put things nicely in proportion when she said, "Here is a misinterpretation of what 'The Method' is supposed to stand for: a man comes on in a scene, very chilly, as if he'd just come from a cold winter's night outdoors. Well, obviously, an actor can't get chilled all the time. He can't put ice cubes down his back. If he's any kind of an actor at all he ought to be able to imagine himself in such a state. If, in the wintertime, the actor was found pacing up and down the theatre alley trying to get cold, with as few clothes on as possible, to make himself ready for his entrance, that to me would be ludicrous and a complete misuse of Stanislavsky's theory. Before, it was all superficial. You were supposed to be possessed of the devil, so you put on one sort of face. You were supposed to be green with envy, so you did another external thing—you clenched your hands, you screwed up your face. But great actors could even make *that* real. Great acting, I feel, is universal, like great music and painting. It's only a 'method' of acting because it's all inside the individual. It's a long course and very difficult, because you have to get to know yourself very well. When I'm given a part to do, I try to fall into some kind of sympathy with the person. The first time I read *I Am a Camera* I had no sympathy with the girl at all. I thought she was a wastrel—foolish, unkind, self-centred, careless, irresponsible. That was my first reaction to Sally Bowles. Well, then I read it again and saw other things in her, which compelled her to behave as she did. And I remembered my own leaving home and my rebellion against a certain kind of life that my family had, which I didn't feel was for me. Then I managed to find a sort of framework for Sally Bowles. So I think, in every part that you do, there is some connection you can make with your own background or with some feeling you've had at one time or another."

Ideally, no doubt, appropriate films should be cast with actors who hold the same principles. A solitary move in this direction was *The Strange One* (1957), advertised as "the first picture filmed entirely by a cast and technicians from The Actors Studio, New York." A splendid bunch they were, too: the players included Gazzara, Peppard, Pat Hingle, Julie Wilson, and James Olson. Even so, the ensemble playing could scarcely bear comparison with the unity of style achieved by Orson Welles when he brought his integrated Mercury Theatre actors to the cinema in *Citizen Kane* over a decade and a half earlier. It was fascinating, too, in the mid-Fifties to see how aptly Welles himself proved *en rapport* with quite a clutch of players from The Actors Studio in *The Long, Hot Summer*: in addition to Newman, that cast included Joanne Woodward and Anthony Franciosa. The presence of Welles in their midst, looming large of course, was a reminder that actors in the U.S.A. and other parts of the world had been discovering their own paths to inner truth. For example, Anna Magnani's association with Italian neo-realism in the Forties, combined with her own superbly vociferous personality, the strong determination that gives way most persuasively to intimations of despair, worked out quite admirably in the sexually charged moments she shared with Franciosa in *Wild Is the Wind* (1957, George Cukor) and Brando in *The Fugitive Kind* (1959, Lumet). Both times, to be sure, the Magnani role was expansive, volatile, impressing us partly by contrast to those around her. Yet Franciosa as the hot-blooded young Basque in *Wild Is the Wind*, arousing and responding to the passion of his foster father's second wife, could really hold the screen with Magnani: no small achievement, especially since her own performance was rich in those small details she endows with the complete illusion of spontaneity, whether exploding with mirth at the sight of a paper cup emerging from a coffee machine or expressing a swift and sympathetic concern for a lassoed stallion as it tumbles to the ground. All this emotion, against the monochrome vastness of a sheep ranch in Nevada (splendid cinematography by Charles Lang), was knowingly controlled by Cukor, of course. The Brando-Magnani confrontations in *The Fugitive Kind*, with Joanne Woodward on hand for good measure as a girl of breeding going to seed, provided another affirmation of identified-acting. On Mississippi soil, Magnani personified those Tennessee Williams yearners: one of the nicest, really, nurturing memories of her father's wine garden which was destroyed mysteriously by fire, tied to humdrum work in a little store, and shackled to a cancer-riddled husband, and all the time so ripe and eager for the physical release that would be granted, transitorily, by the fugitive who was also destined for burning, leaving behind an exuberant memory to set beside others . . . and a snakeskin jacket to be donned for a time, perhaps, by another of his own kind. It was less remarkable that Brando, especially in such an impressive role, should have dominated this film than that Franciosa could meet the Magnani fire in *Wild Is the Wind*. His was the second male lead: Magnani was already matched by a leading actor of size, Anthony Quinn as the foster father of Franciosa; and Quinn, of course, had notable acquaintance with Italian neo-realism in Fellini's *La strada* (1954). As it turned out, Franciosa's career in Hollywood never provided a similar chance to demonstrate the full capacity of his talent, but in this specific movie, which might have degenerated into meretricious stuff quite easily, the young actor not only rose to the emotional peaks of his experienced elders but also made it clear that The Actors Studio could give its members the ability to accommodate their personal interpretations in company with fine players whose realism had been learned elsewhere.

A fundamental affinity could be traced back over the years, as was evident in Magnani's first Hollywood movie *The Rose Tattoo* (1955). There she was partnered, astoundingly well, by Burt Lancaster. A singular item, really: of special interest in this context as an instance of "being" rather than "acting," with the additional problem of characters who were larger than life. Yet another film of a play by Tennessee Williams, it was shrewdly modulated for cinema by Daniel Mann, the same director who had guided its Broadway production in which the leading roles were played by Maureen Stapleton and Eli Wallach. In a village on the Gulf Coast, some distance from New Orleans, the Sicilian widow Serafina (Magnani) positively writhed in desire for her dead husband, a man whose animal virility had been blended with a poetic grace exemplified by the rose tattoo on his chest, an ornamentation curiously duplicated upon the torso of a truck driver who happened to be stranded in town and served as something near enough to a reincarnation of Serafina's departed spouse. The pathos, somewhat overwrought, and tenuously metaphorical, was balanced nimbly by a broad humour to which Magnani gave a tragi-comic extravagance that was very nearly equalled by the pyrotechnics of Lancaster as the truck driver. A simpleton, an exaggerated case of the nomad-stud, this man required great finesse in the playing and Lancaster was the actor to provide it. Indeed, as he had indicated from the beginning of his

Hollywood career as the muscular and apprehensive Swede in *The Killers* (1946, Robert Siodmak), he could be a star personality and an interior actor as well, simultaneously if necessary but mostly by alternatives. In the Fifties one found him spoofing the swashbucklers with panache in Siodmak's *The Crimson Pirate* (1952) and other perky romps, but doing the chameleon trick with the best of them in such realistic characterisations as the down-at-heel chiropractor in *Come Back, Little Sheba* (also 1952; Daniel Mann) and the vicious columnist in *Sweet Smell of Success* (1957, Alexander Mackendrick). Indeed, Lancaster typifies the development in the Fifties from an emphasis upon the personality star to a wary but steadily increasing appreciation of the actor. His is a heightened case, perhaps; but it throws light upon this period of transition. Formerly a circus acrobat, he came to the movies with a disciplined physical strength and the grace of a panther. His rugged features were not conducive to the glamour-boy image that impeded, to some extent, such capable performers as Cornel Wilde and Tony Curtis. Lancaster's proclivity for identification, however, dated back to his youth: "Before the circus and vaudeville, I worked for many years as an amateur in reproductions of Broadway plays at a settlement house in the neighbourhood where I was born in New York City. I was very fortunate, because at that time there was a professional group in New York called the American Laboratory Theatre. Its director was Richard Boleslawski. And part of the training they underwent was to send their people to various settlement houses in the poorer areas of the city and have them teach, and direct amateur performances. So I did have something of a background when I first went into the theatre and then into films."

Polish-born, Boleslawski had been at the Moscow Art Theatre when the Stanislavsky theories were being put into practice. His later work as a Hollywood director in the Thirties brought established stars under his wing, with extremely varied results: a bunch of Barrymores in *Rasputin and the Empress,* Garbo in *The Painted Veil,* Laughton and March in *Les Misérables,* Dietrich and Boyer in *The Garden of Allah.* None of those instances would have suggested a major reformation. They serve rather to suggest that a certain size, inherited from the

Opposite: Shirley Booth—(above, left) in HOT SPELL, and (right) with Lancaster in COME BACK, LITTLE SHEBA. (Below) Gazzara as the sadist in THE STRANGE ONE

theatre, was allied to identification with character by the best of those star performers, and that The Actors Studio in its own era used the Stanislavsky philosophy as a basis which could be adapted to a changing idea of realism. Just as manners change with the years, so does the actor's art which reflects his own period in history, or draws parallels between the "now" he knows about and the past he studies for a work that is not set in "the present." One assumes that there was a subtle variation in style between the mid-Forties classes at The Actors Studio and the famous Group Theatre of the Thirties in which both Strasberg and Kazan were very much involved.

There were other roads to truth in characterisation, of course. A strong influence at the Neighbourhood Playhouse in New York was the choreographer Martha Graham. She and members of her dance company gave instruction in movement to Playhouse actors, and the Graham system was derived from the precepts of her medical father, a specialist in mental diseases. As Martha Graham recalls it, "He told me when I was a child that movement did not lie, that sooner or later you would reveal yourself by some movement of the body. A shrug of the shoulders can mean that you're insecure. The shoulders of an assured person will have a perfect tranquillity. The principal thing is not to make all of those fluttery movements which are such a screen for what really goes on inside you. Most of us are concerned not with revealing what we feel but with hiding what we feel." An application of this line of thinking influenced the comic and yet realistic manifestations of neurosis in the acting of Tony Randall, who gravitated to Hollywood in the late Fifties and was both funny and true in *No Down Payment* and *Pillow Talk*. Conversely, the Graham principles inform the quietude, the economy of movement, every gesture serving a purpose, every thought written in the eyes, of Gregory Peck whose Neighbourhood Playhouse experience prepared him to lend conviction, sometimes against considerable odds, to a variety of Hollywood films of which the best in the Fifties were *The Gunfighter, Roman Holiday,* and especially John Huston's *Moby Dick* (1956) in which his wonderfully understated portrayal of the obsessed Captain Ahab was an object lesson in acting inside the head; he did fall foul, however, of a mawkish concept of the hapless F. Scott Fitzgerald in *Beloved Infidel* (1959, directed by Henry King who was equally thrown by a turgid screenplay and a superfluity of Cinema-Scope).

142

There were also those who found their way to identification by dint of experience and personal application. The trouper's route to Hollywood, and to performances that owed much to instinct, was taken by Shirley Booth. A middle-aged arrival in 1952, she rang so true as Lola in *Come Back, Little Sheba* that one might have supposed her background to be one of dedicated improvisation in a most advanced school of acting. In fact it was the outcome of hard slogging in stock companies, plus the bread-and-butter stint of a popular radio series, *Duffy's Tavern*. Her interpretation of the slovenly, good-hearted but irritating Lola, letting herself and her marriage go to pieces, mindlessly, unintentionally, carrying on about her lost dog "Little Sheba" which symbolises the lost *joie de vivre* that will never return however much she wishes, was evidently foreign to her nature. The sloppy housekeeping, so humorously and yet pathetically portrayed, required a *volte face* in her own estimation: "I'm just the opposite. I'm a fanatic about the house. When I should be studying French, I'm cleaning out closets and drawers. I'm one of these people who spend hours doing something and in five minutes can upset the whole thing and start all over again. I just like to straighten things, and that's a far cry from Lola. I'm what you'd call a comfortable person, and I knew that if I were ever going to get anywhere in films it would have to be as one of those comfortable sort of square people —I mean in figure, not in character." One must remember, however, that her Broadway success as Lola and her modification of the role for the closer range of the film camera were both directed by Daniel Mann, one of the directors who took classes at The Actors Studio. Obviously he was not only aware of the considerable differences between theatre and cinema, but capable of negotiating the necessary fining down which never comes easily to a player who must virtually minimise a characterisation that has been projected to reach the back rows night after night. "Doing a moving picture," said Shirley Booth, "is like telling a very personal experience to someone in your own living room. You don't have to project so much but it's just as powerful: the atom bomb is pretty small, too. There was a moment in the play when I'm telephoning my mother, and on the stage I would lower my head to express emotion, but in pictures the close-up camera was right there, so really the movie audience were in on the emotional secrets, more than the people in the theatre." Daniel Mann directed all but one of her four Hollywood films; and the other, *The*

Matchmaker, was directed by Joseph Anthony, another Actors Studio man. In fact, the William Inge play and the Thornton Wilder farce, each with its mutations of humour and sadness, brought out the best in Shirley Booth; although her value was still apparent in the sentimental mire of *About Mrs. Leslie* (1953), wherein she gave a certain elusive charm to a loquacious ex-showbiz type who became a kept woman in California and tried, after her lover's death, to make the most of a humdrum existence; and, setting aside a fleeting "guest" appearance in a trifle called *Main Street to Broadway,* she was able to win hearts and furtive tears in *Hot Spell* (1958) as the long-suffering mother of a tiresome family in Louisiana, staunchly backed by a strong cast including Anthony Quinn, Shirley MacLaine, Earl Holliman and Eileen Heckart. Even when the material took some cracking, Shirley Booth did more than was necessary, showing never a sign of effort. But, in view of the directors concerned, it might be said that the Stanislavsky spirit had something to do with it.

Sceptics denigrated The Actors Studio repeatedly, and while its influence upon Hollywood increased there was a minor tendency for publicists to draw attention to the fact that some up-and-coming young star had no association whatever with "The Method." This carried some weight in the cases of two decidedly good players who had found other paths to their goal and could both have claimed, had they chosen to do so, to have acting in their blood: they were James MacArthur (son of Helen Hayes) who made an auspicious film *début* in Frankenheimer's *The Young Stranger* (1957) but then frittered away the rest of the decade in harmless but uninteresting Disney trifles, and Anthony Perkins (son of Osgood Perkins) who gangled disarmingly in Cukor's *The Actress* (1953) and soon became established as one of the very best interior actors, especially after his brilliant performance in Mulligan's *Fear Strikes Out* (1957).

However, if The Actors Studio needed a justification, it could hardly have been furnished with a more telling example than Marilyn Monroe. The archetypal sexpot, she had pottered to no great effect through minor roles in Hollywood at the end of the Forties and then had impinged suddenly on Mankiewicz's *All about Eve* and Huston's *The*

Opposite: Marilyn Monroe—with Tom Ewell (above) in THE SEVEN YEAR ITCH; with Don Murray, Hope Lange and Betty Field (below) in BUS STOP

145

Asphalt Jungle, both in 1950. From there on she ascended rapidly as a pleasing eyeful, her reach exceeding her grasp quite often, as in Henry Hathaway's melodramatic *Niagara* (1953) where her potential as a *femme fatale* in the old tradition but with a refreshing shape was no more than sufficient to compete with the scenery. At her best, as in a lighter movie of the same year, *Gentlemen Prefer Blondes* (Howard Hawks), she was a delightful star personality: no more, but certainly no less. Then in 1955, directed by Billy Wilder and partnered by an Actors Studio performer, Tom Ewell, she managed to underline sexy humour with a certain pathos as the girl who stimulates a grass widower suffering from *The Seven Year Itch.* After this film was completed, Marilyn Monroe spent a considerable time in New York at The Actors Studio, where her special mentors were Lee Strasberg and his wife Paula. A deal of mock was made about this, but sneers were eradicated when the results were seen in Joshua Logan's *Bus Stop* (1956): a glamour girl had been transmuted—an actress was to hand. Not merely the performance of her career, superior by far to anything else in the two dozen movies she made during the Fifties, her interpretation of Cherie, a floozy with ideals above her immediate station as a *chanteuse* at a Phenix night club, was quaint, touching, forlorn, sadly funny to just the right degree, and so genuinely felt as to rank among the best performances of the decade. The character was beautifully conceived initially by William Inge; Kim Stanley had played the part on Broadway. And George Axelrod's screenplay opened out the action, incorporating scenes in the night club and at a rodeo before settling into the single locale of the play, a bar-restaurant where a busload of people are compelled to wait for an unknown period of time on account of a heavy snowfall. At the same time, Axelrod preserved the sensitivity of Inge, and the delicate blending of knock-about mirth and fundamental insecurity. Cherie harboured dreams of progressing from her origins in the Ozarks to stardom in Hollywood. Forestalled by declarations of love and an offer of marriage by a lusty young cowboy (eloquently played by Don Murray), Cherie sees her ambitions dwindling, her future reduced to mere domesticity on a ranch in Montana. She resists. He persists. And from this absurdly simple premise, a wealth of human conflict arises. The problem of choice, between an ideal that might well prove shallow, and a chance of security that might eventually become dull. It is fear, and a deal of affection for the blunt and honest cowboy, that win Cherie over at last, after strong protestations and a mutual exhaustion that brings their two heads to rest sideways across the bar (in a splendidly apt composition for CinemaScope). And beneath all the merriment, and the well sustained twang to her voice, Marilyn Monroe was no longer the sex symbol who had delighted night-out audiences and commercial Hollywood hearts. She had learned how to inhabit a role, and she inhabited Cherie. This girl was real and true. As Joshua Logan remarked, "She made it almost a Chaplinesque figure. She saw that in it, and she knew just what she was doing." And in the doing of it, she signified a demarcation between the old Hollywood and the new American cinema, in which "star" would no longer be either a guarantee of financial returns or a token of esteem. Already many a celebrity of the movies had let it be known that actor or actress was a preferable term, implying talent, whereas "star" can mean nothing more than magnetism. Of course, Marilyn Monroe had that as well. But in *Bus Stop* she had more: not for long, regrettably—she died in 1962—but for long enough to let us know that, even for a "star," the dividing line between acting and being could disappear.

7. Showbiz Neurosis

THE GLAMOUR OF SHOW BUSINESS and of stardom was still perpetuated in many films that augmented the backstage tears and on-stage smiles of previous decades with the visual and audible onslaughts of big-scale productions. Yet, parallel with this tradition, a stronger impact was made by movies that observed the underbelly of show business, in Hollywood and in other areas of entertainment, acknowledging more frequently than in the past that the display of glamour often masked an erosion of the spirit. In a season of anxiety, it was apt that the year 1950 should have yielded not only *Sunset Boulevard,* casting a jaundiced eye upon Hollywood *Angst,* but also *All about Eve* which derided the back-biters of Broadway.

Ironically, the story of Billy Wilder's *Sunset Boulevard* was told by a dead man. The corpse of a screenplay writer, Joe Gillis (William Holden), floated face-down upon the surface of a swimming pool.

From deep in the water, the camera observed this hulk of expendable humanity, which gave disembodied voice to a first-person narration. The tale was partly about himself, a victim of compromise between art and financial expediency, and it was equally about the grandiose star in eclipse, Norma Desmond (Gloria Swanson), whose heyday in the silent Twenties was wishfully recalled by the furnishings and ambiance of the ivory tower mansion she was still wealthy enough to inhabit. In 1950, it was not entirely uncommon for stars to venture forth in cars lined with tiger skin, as Norma Desmond did, but Wilder presented her as a woman dedicated to myth, living near to hallucination all the time. Nostalgically, yet with an absurd *hauteur,* she viewed herself when younger on a private screen, attended and protected by a white-gloved butler (Erich von Stroheim). It was this man, we learned, who had directed her silent films and had ensured her present economic security. The writer Gillis was trapped in this household by his personal lack of security, living virtually as a kept man as he tried to think up a screenplay that would serve for Norma Desmond's comeback. Like the writer himself, this project was doomed.

Pertinently, in view of the new financial pressures, *Sunset Boulevard* reminded us of the panic which had beset Hollywood some twenty years previously when the advent of sound had caused a disruption as confounding as the arrival now of strong competition from television. Norma Desmond had survived the Depression years that, coupled with the switch to talkies, brought many stars to their knees. Her attempted suicide was prompted by the realisation, at last, that her day was done; and Billy Wilder conveyed her tragic self-discovery in a dramatic shot of her hands clutching at a bedstead, the slashed wrists bandaged, the arms reaching up and the fingers clawing to some tangible contact.

Realisation came more swiftly to the Broadway actress Margo Channing (Bette Davis) in *All about Eve.* Firmly established in the New York theatre, she had much need of praise nevertheless, as do so many in her ephemeral profession. So she responded warmly at first to the blandishments of Eve (Anne Baxter), a younger woman who ventured to admire her in wide-eyed humility, and, telling a tale of woe, moved the actress to employ her as a secretary. From there on, Eve's outward charm worked overtime in the interest of her steely ambition. Opportunism was her speciality. Beguiling Margo

Channing's friends, Eve got her chance as an actress at the expense of her benefactor, who was sophisticated enough to catch on quickly but was unable to forestall her rival's progress. To add a bitter taste at the end, as well as to imply that the rules of the game are dirty, Eve herself was flattered persuasively at the height of triumph by another young girl whose motives were identical to her own. Joseph L. Mankiewicz, who wrote and directed the film, surrounded this last girl with mirrors, to which she bowed in duplicate imagery, suggesting, as Mankiewicz put it, "a multiplicity of Eves." *All about Eve* was especially strong in its dialogue, balancing the moral stricture with an astringent wit.

Similar elements of *Angst* in Hollywood and New York were present

The rules of the game are dirty—Anne Baxter, Bette Davis, Marilyn Monroe and George Sanders in ALL ABOUT EVE

"Great. Until she met her match—the bottle." JEANNE EAGELS (Kim Novak, right) is entrusted by Elsie Desmond (Virginia Grey) with the script of RAIN

in Stuart Heisler's *The Star* (1952) and George Sidney's *Jeanne Eagels* (1957). With Bette Davis at fuller throttle, *The Star* was a moist lament for a movie actress who lived nearer to earth than Norma Desmond. This one's career was only just going into decline, and so were her resources at the bank. Egocentric and temperamental, she battled to regain her status, surrendering intermittently to the bottle and to self-pity, but mustering the grit to try her skill as a shop assistant when funds were short. It was perhaps a truer, if more sentimental, portrait than *Sunset Boulevard* provided with Norma Desmond. Like the other Bette Davis character, Margo Channing, this star retreated eventually from the rat-race with tolerable decorum, settling for marriage to a patient open-air type (Sterling Hayden), who had been waiting for her to get the stardust out of her system. Jeanne Eagels, on the other hand (a real-life figure, this: possibly moulded to the movie's purposes), took the relentless course and died of it. As ruthless as Eve (according to the screenplay, at any rate), Jeanne Eagels became a celebrity on Broadway in the Twenties.

The incidents which brought Eve to mind, and also brought out the best in Sidney's direction, outlined the tactics Jeanne Eagels employed to gain for herself the Somerset Maugham play *Rain*. She was at this time, we gathered, a fairly promising young actress who had been given her first lead in a play that was doing badly on its pre-Broadway tour. During this fretful period of try-out performances and script-doctoring, a fallen Broadway star, Elsie Desmond (Virginia Grey), approached Jeanne Eagels in the lobby of an hotel, thrusting into her hands a script of *Rain* and asking the fashionable newcomer to persuade her impresario to consider it as a comeback vehicle for the older actress. Already evaded by the impresario, Elsie Desmond had to swallow her pride, and a tranquilliser, before she could make this pitiful request. Jeanne Eagels gave every sign of sympathy. Nobody overheard their conversation. But the encounter was observed from a distance by Jeanne's dramatic coach, Mme. Neilson (played by Agnes Moorehead with that formidable ferocity that typifies certain women who thrive on the periphery of theatre life). Mme. Neilson informed Jeanne that Elsie Desmond had indeed been a fine actress: "She was great. Until she met her match—the bottle." This piece of gossip, coupled with the small white pill we had seen the ex-star gulping down, prefigured the future of Jeanne herself and of numerous other stars, both real and fictitious, whose careers were popular grist to Hollywood's voracious mill throughout the Fifties. Jeanne read *Rain* and told the impresario that it was an infinitely better work than the play they were doing. He agreed that it would be ideal for Jeanne, but he was concerned about Elsie Desmond's rights in the matter, which Jeanne brushed aside with the assurance that the other actress had virtually made her a present of the play.

It is true that *Rain,* with Jeanne Eagels as Sadie Thompson, enjoyed a long run on Broadway in the Twenties. How much relationship to fact can be found in the movie's representation of the New York opening night, I cannot tell. But the sequence was superb. Rain was actually falling as the audience scurried into the theatre beneath a marquee bearing the play's title. Backstage, Jeanne Eagels was standing in the wings, ready to make her entrance. It was dark there—but some light from the stage, together with her stark white make-up and heavily shaded eyelids, gave her face a hardness. The tension beneath that mask of make-up was palpable. Then, in a breathtaking shock effect, a figure emerged from the dark beside her. Elsie Desmond was also in the wings, swooping upon her usurper, hissing venom, decreeing that the play would bring Jeanne Eagels luck undoubtedly —"all of it bad." The contrast between the dissipated face of Elsie Desmond in the half light and the terror beneath the Jeanne Eagels mask had a muted expressionist style, which Sidney repeated at other key points in a film that used black-and-white photography for a variety of chiaroscuro effects.

For Sidney the movie was quite a departure. His customary field was the competent glamour movie, chiefly the musical. In 1950, for example, he had directed an efficient screen version of *Annie Get Your Gun* with its star-dusty assertion that "show people . . smile when they are low." Sidney must have been well aware that, while this might be true of some resilient individuals, it was far from common. "Show people" are a nervy lot, whether low or high.

Jeanne Eagels collapsed on stage after too much drinking followed by dope (or so the movie had it). This pattern was repeated through films of the Fifties and beyond, almost compulsively: the artist as manic-depressive, in cinema or any other medium, was studied remorselessly.

It was usually easier to contemplate movies like this when the characters were fictitious. More seemly, of course: also, smacking less of the gloat at a real person's misery, the fictitious plot would tend to be constructed with more freedom and consequently more realism. Even Bing Crosby, in one of his rare departures from laughter and light, played a showbiz alcoholic quite credibly in *The Country Girl* (1954), directed by George Seaton and adapted from the play of the same name by Clifford Odets (in this case the play, but not the film, had its title changed to *Winter Journey* for presentation in the U.K., presumably to avoid confusion with an old musical comedy called *The Country Girl*). This was undoubtedly a work that owed its persuasion to fiction. Without the embarrassment of real-life associations, the weak central figure struggling to gain enough self-respect to attempt a comeback was immediately sympathetic, but he was also seen to be tiresome to his wife and the friend who tried to help him. These two equally important characters were played extremely well by Grace Kelly and William Holden. The wife, whose fortitude was a constant reproach to her husband's folly, gradually dominated the plot and drew attention to the personality scars that result from a luckless marriage. So, while the showbiz drunk himself was to a large extent similar to the mainly feminine instances from real life that were set before us so often, the film's fiction carried a stronger illusion of truth than most other movies in this vein.

The general advantages of fiction, which could be related to reality, were evident again in John Cromwell's *The Goddess* (1958), a film

Personality scars—THE COUNTRY GIRL played by Grace Kelly (left); and (right) Kim Stanley with Lloyd Bridges in THE GODDESS

153

that probably benefited as well from being made in New York and elsewhere, away from the pressures of Hollywood itself. The screenplay by Paddy Chayefsky was a distinct advance upon the average run of movies about the movie queen who arrived from nowhere, the small town girl who made it big in Hollywood but whose life of ease and wealth began swiftly to mingle with a steady intake of liquor and tranquillisers until her spirit, already feeble, cracked at the graveside of her neglectful mother. Given Chayefsky's dialogue and a notable interior performance by Kim Stanley, the grains of truth that lurk in every cliché seemed grittier than usual. The anti-heroine's hysterical laughter during the funeral ceremony was not merely an attack upon false conventions but a core of the theme: the display of status, the keeping up of appearances, became too great a burden for a small personality that had been inflated by the cinema's publicity machine, and the lure of the bitch-goddess—"Success."

Such essays on spiritual corruption as an outcome of material success were occasionally placed in other spheres, especially the world of big business, as in Robert Wise's *Executive Suite* (1954); but it was within the myth-circle of show business that inward-looking American films discovered their most frequent examples, which began to take on the quality of allegory as the decade continued.

The thought was more abounding, but of course it wasn't new. One of the best-known variations, George Cukor's *A Star Is Born* (1954) was a re-make of William Wellman's 1937 movie of the same name, saying the same things, which were far more daring to say in the Thirties. That initial version, starring Fredric March and Janet Gaynor, was a rare thing in its day: Hollywood going in for self-criticism, washing its dirty linen on the screen. The story was, in both cases, of two stars, man and wife, whose domestic life suffered because the woman grew more popular than her husband. He declined into drunken depression and committed suicide in romantic style, both times, by walking across a beach and deeper and deeper and deeper into the ocean. The Cukor version was played by James Mason and Judy Garland, who was on top form in a long bravura speech, brimful of pity for her husband and herself, eloquently sustained in a single take, the pathos accentuated just sufficiently by the clownish make-up she was wearing as she spoke: a dressing room speech, indeed, the quintessence of showbiz *Angst*.

Cukor in the previous year, 1953, had made a more delicate film called *The Actress,* depicting the star-urge in its formative phase. The lure of footlights was the elementary motivation; Jean Simmons was charming as the young girl who sat enthralled in a theatre, watching a musical show. "Beautiful Lady," sang the people on the stage (certain cinemas of the period splayed out to wide-screen for this sequence), and the girl wanted to be a beautiful lady herself. *The Actress* was really a domestic comedy, with Spencer Tracy as an affectionate if grumpish father; but, in the context of showbiz cinema, it had a special place, redressing the balance a little by suggesting that adjustment and survival were feasible for some. It had the asset of hindsight, because it was based upon the early life of its writer, Ruth Gordon, who adapted it from her stage play *Years Ago.* She was well and truly established by the Fifties as an actress of idiosyncratic wit and tremendous charm, known best in the theatre but also popping up in the occasional film, and doing very nicely always. She wrote with great humour as well, often in collaboration with her husband Garson Kanin; and screenplays by the Kanins were often filmed by Cukor. Therefore, at the fade-out of *The Actress,* when the girl left home with paternal blessing to pursue her dream of theatrical glory, there was an upbeat ending justified by what happened to Ruth Gordon as life went on. This in itself set the film apart from the two parallel categories of glossy fame-overnight and squalid agony. At the same time, one could never have called *The Actress* a cosy work. Ruth Gordon's astringent mind cut through the implicit sentimentality with lightly satiric humour, making fair game of the small town mentality. It had, of course, the quaintness of a period piece, set in the Twenties; but psychologically it was valid for any period. The film had an incidental point of interest because it marked the first movie appearance of Anthony Perkins as the girl's racoon-coated beau, a figure of fun and of diffident charm. In fact, it was charm, an elusive quality, which permeated the movie and made it something of an object lesson. The process of persuading the father that a career on the stage would be all right was the daughter's major problem, and what emerged convincingly was the father's understanding. In his youth he had known the tug of adventure himself, and had taken the obvious escape route by going to sea. Now, firmly entrenched in family life, he remembered how he had felt and knew exactly how his daughter

felt. There was a true and unstressed emotion to the final shot, after he had presented her with a telescope as a good luck token, and she left the house while the camera remained in the room that had sheltered her: through the window she could be seen, going her way bravely while the music of "Beautiful Lady" welled up on the soundtrack. Banality was transcended, by the writing and the acting and Cukor's astute direction.

While *The Actress* stood aside, the welter of downbeat films continued to enlist our sympathy and concern for the showfolk. But Hollywood also took into account the kind of star who is not born but made, in more senses than one. This was partly the point of *The Goddess,* and entirely the topic of a delightful comedy (written, incidentally, by Garson Kanin) called *The Girl Can't Help It* (1956). Directed with evident relish by Frank Tashlin, it had Edmond O'Brien as a loud-mouthed caricature-gangster whose diversions included a wry reminder of Norma Desmond's nostalgic viewings of her old movies: this well-heeled hood had his home-movies too—ancient newsreels of his numerous arrests that gave him a sense of importance. At his bidding, Tom Ewell set about promoting the gangster's moll as a night club celebrity. The girl had no talent but this was seen to be of trivial consequence in view of her eminent bust, her incredibly nipped-in waist, and her generous hip-span. Nobody since Mae West in the Thirties had come so close to resembling a magnified egg-timer. The part was played with hilarious mock-innocence by Jayne Mansfield. Nonetheless *The Girl Can't Help It* bore signs of uncertainty. Satire, however broad, was a dubious proposition for Hollywood; and the movie was interrupted by frenetic songs from sundry pop stars as Ewell led the girl from one nightspot to another in order to catch the eyes of potential employers. Where Tashlin and Kanin and Jayne Mansfield really scored were in the numerous unabashed demonstrations of the instant stardom that can be attained by physical allure and nothing else. One swift sequence, early in the film, showed the girl tittuping along a street and thereby causing ice to turn to water beneath the iceman's sweating palm, and milk to boil and bubble in a bottle held by a spellbound milkman; symbolism was never more explicit, nor stardom more assured.

Opposite: Anthony Perkins and Jean Simmons in
THE ACTRESS

The actress-star with a true sense of vocation, on the other hand, was best represented in the Fifties by a re-make of a 1933 film, *Morning Glory,* which had been one of Katharine Hepburn's earliest movies. The 1958 version, *Stage Struck* (a back-stepping title, indeed), was the third and most demanding of Susan Strasberg's film appearances. Critical eyes were upon her, not only because of Hepburn memories, but more especially because, as the daughter of Lee Strasberg, founder of The Actors Studio, she aroused much speculation. A semblance of the improvisation for which The Actors Studio was noted could scarcely have been provided better, as it turned out, than in the famous theatrical party scene where the girl, nearly starving and slightly tipsy from champagne taken on an empty stomach, regales the host and distinguished guests with a portion of the balcony scene from *Romeo and Juliet.* Every Katharine Hepburn admirer knew this double-test well, and Susan Strasberg came through nobly. Over the years, the story remained surprisingly fresh. The director, Sidney Lumet, was fairly new to cinema, and his previous movie *Twelve Angry Men* had retained the claustrophobic setting of its origin as TV drama. In *Stage Struck,* Lumet expanded. Filming entirely in New York, he made sparkling use of colour photography and realistic but sufficiently poetic locations, such as Greenwich Village where the girl scraped a living for a time by reciting poetry in a bistro, and legendary places like Sardi's Restaurant and the Martin Beck Theatre.

It was a film well provided with players: Henry Fonda as a Broadway producer, Christopher Plummer as an edgy playwright, Herbert Marshall as a veteran actor, and Joan Greenwood as an exceedingly grand star. This last was a superbly muted caricature, really; and a highlight of the film was Joan Greenwood's feline sex-and-finance scene with Fonda, their kisses punctuated with such remarks as "What would you think of seven-fifty a week?" Meanwhile, the central figure of the up and coming young actress, unquestionably dedicated, was a fascinating study to place beside others that have been noted in this chapter. While sympathetic, she was nevertheless obliged to connive, less ruthlessly than the ambitious girls in *All about Eve* and *Jeanne Eagels,* but sufficiently to imply again that progress in the theatre demanded a certain sacrifice of scruples. In private she rehearsed a star part in a new play, intended to be a vehicle for the Joan Greenwood character, whose temperament was wearing everybody down. The girl had the incidental advantage, as well, of sexual appeal for the producer and the playwright, and note was taken of this—but primarily, we gathered, it was her talent which earned her the big chance when the star left a rehearsal in a huff. Here we had the valid *cliché,* of course: equally valid in some cases, no doubt, would be the girl's ultimate rejection of love on the grounds that an actress must be wedded to the theatre.

Questions of motivation, and of dedication too, were raised more intriguingly in a lesser film, *Man of a Thousand Faces* (1957, Joseph Pevney). The style was conventional, but the subject was compulsive: it examined the life and career of Lon Chaney, whose horrific character studies in films of the Twenties have earned their niche among the classics, quaint though they look when resurrected today. The fascinating thing about Chaney was that exhibitionism could hardly have been his spur. His great talent was not for projecting his own personality, but for concealing it beneath disguises. This is the antithesis of the star image, although it can be related to childhood games, dressing up, getting temporarily inside the skin of another creature and then returning contented to the real world in time for tea. Chaney was portrayed, inappropriately but gamely, by a well established star with a strong image of his own, James Cagney. An unknown would have aided credibility, but the tale, as told, was engrossing all the same. According to the film, Chaney's aptitude for physical permutations was not at first an instinctive thing, but simply a means to an end. He needed money badly to support his young son Creighton, after a divorce from his first wife. The circumstances were as harrowing as any depicted in the most downbeat of the showbiz biographies. Dorothy Malone churned one's stomach as the first Mrs. Chaney, whose neurotic behaviour was partially explained by the shock she received upon discovering that both of her husband's parents were deaf and dumb; she feared that the child she was carrying might inherit this misfortune. And, although her anxiety proved unfounded when the boy was born, her unsteady nerves, combined with a taste for more pleasure than domesticity permitted, sent her loping down the primrose path. Chaney was a vaudeville artist at the time, and his wife didn't help his career by drinking acid on the stage in the middle of his act: this enabled Dorothy Malone to do some very impressive croaking when she returned in the later phases of the film.

After these pertinent but exhaustive preliminaries, the ingenuity of Chaney was illustrated quite absorbingly. To make ends meet, he began work as a silent movie extra at Universal. (In fact, *Man of a Thousand Faces* was presented by Universal as its Golden Jubilee Film; although Universal's pride in its past was undermined slightly here by the necessary recognition of Chaney's departure to M-G-M, where the young Irving Thalberg was portrayed as the nicest possible guy—and was acted by Robert J. Evans, an actor who eventually switched from unremarkable thespian activities to become a production chief at Paramount.) Chaney discovered at Universal that extras were cast to type, but his speed and inventive prowess with the make-up kit transformed him into figures of any nationality or age. He worked at this game prodigiously, to gain enough money to prove to legal authorities that he was capable of giving his son a good home: Creighton, meanwhile, was in an orphanage, and the wife had vanished. (One wondered incessantly if all this could be entirely true; but it was a tremendous impression of doing things the hard way.) The highlight of this silent movie phase, and indeed of the entire film, showed Chaney undertaking the part of a cripple, so distorted of limb that he had virtually to crawl into camera range, where he seemed to draw instinctively upon the sign language he had used as a child to communicate with his parents. He was bandaged painfully to assume these grotesque contortions. When the director called "Cut," the assembled cast and crew gave him a spontaneous round of applause. A star was born in agony.

From there on, the film suggested that dedication was added to Chaney's drive. Reconstructions were made of specific scenes from his movies, including *The Hunchback of Notre Dame* and *The Phantom of the Opera,* and for these passages the face of James Cagney could be as thoroughly disguised as Chaney's had been in the originals. The feeling that a good deal more than expediency was involved as his career progressed was very emphatic in the death scene. He handed his son Creighton his make-up box with the name Lon Chaney written upon it, and, as a last inspirational gesture, the dying man added a "Jr." after the name. Creighton was played, however, by Roger Smith, a personable young actor who became popular in the Sixties as a star of the TV series *77 Sunset Strip.* He looked unlikely to grow up into the rugged Lon Chaney Jr., whose face was familiar already to moviegoers of the Fifties, mostly in lesser horror movies than had come his father's way, and sometimes even in comedy-horror of small merit, although he proved at least twice (as Lennie in *Of Mice and Men* in 1939, and as an ex-convict in *The Defiant Ones* in 1958) that, given the chance to be serious, he could act extremely well.

The enigma that remained at the end of *Man of a Thousand Faces* was exactly why, after the initial financial purpose had been served, Chaney developed the compulsion to go on submitting himself to physical constrictions that endangered his health. His attitude, as depicted, seemed akin to that of the mountaineer who heads for the most dangerous peak, pitting himself against nature: a traditional challenge, of course, and one which at least is not necessarily harmful to others, but nevertheless an excess too readily honoured, and fundamentally as disturbing as most manifestations of extreme will-power and courage.

The same thoughts were provoked by George Marshall's *Houdini* (1953), a realism-in-aspic treatment of the famous escapologist's private life but, intermittently, a film well above the showbiz glamour level when it gave a glimpse (however true or false) of an obsessive mentality. It has been said that Harry Houdini, like other magicians of note, relied upon tricks. He was endowed with great physical strength, which he augmented by rigorous training. Beyond this, the movie gave intimations, in its best passages, of an almost superhuman will-power. There was an extraordinary sequence at the Astor Hotel in New York, where a society of magicians were celebrating Halloween with an annual banquet, and volunteers were called upon to worm their way out of straight jackets. While everybody who came forward was seen to stumble about in the constricting bonds, the young and unknown Houdini remained perfectly still, concentrating upon a point of light in the chandelier, sweat breaking out on his face, until eventually the fingers of one hand emerged from confinement, as if by an act of will the arm had grown beyond its normal length. Obviously, in cinema, it was an easy thing to do. But Marshall timed his shots and built his tension so well that the scene became mesmerising, even frightening; and the same quality was regained whenever the screenplay dwelt upon the man's determination to increase his abilities.

The film's story, for all its gloss, was often diverting. It began with Houdini's early struggles, before the turn of the century. There was a good light-corny beginning at a carnival, where he snarled in a

cage, got up as Bruto the Wild Man, gaining the half-terrified pity of a schoolgirl who eventually became his wife—and was awakened from sleep on the wedding night to be sawn in half, because her husband's experimental compulsions had to be indulged at whatever moment they happened to strike him. Interwoven with such frivolities was a darker strain, linked to superstition. Halloween was considered an unlucky time for Houdini, yet it was the appointed date for one of his most dangerous exploits—an immersion in the freezing waters of the Detroit River while incarcerated in a padlocked box. A hint of his preparation for this escape was given in a lighter episode: a bath in his hotel suite was laden with quantities of ice, brought in by astonished waiters who were requested to pour more and more upon his shivering body, much to the consternation of his ever-clucking spouse (Janet Leigh). The feat itself developed into a protracted, and perfectly judged, sequence of suspense. The casket was lowered through a big hole in the ice, which otherwise stretched all over the surface of the river. Houdini broke loose as planned and drifted from the casket, up to the barrier of thick ice. But he could not locate the gap in the surface. Airless time went by as he moved beneath the heavy layer of ice. A cut to the anxious crowd above: some desperate, unsuccessful work with grappling hooks. Houdini's wife fainted and was taken away. The crowd dispersed. Night came. And then, in a memorable frame, the dark hole in the ice was guarded by a solitary figure, Houdini's German assistant and latterday mentor (Torin Thatcher).

One felt that the actual event could not possibly have been so prolonged as they made it in the film. But that single image of the waiting man, exerting some wishful power of his own, went beyond hokum: it held a dark strength. The implications of supernatural powers were neatly judged, merging with the practical-seeming quest by Houdini for the greatest trick of all. The mystic quality was unexpectedly pronounced in certain moments. Tony Curtis played Houdini, and it had been no surprise to find him moving nimbly from the initial lightness of mood to the routine domestic and emotional passages; and his athletic physique, if lacking the musculature indicated by photographs of the real Houdini, was suited to the film's purpose

Opposite: Tony Curtis as HOUDINI

of suggesting a flexibility which, allied to mental concentration, could enable such a man to open a prison door with his foot, picking the lock with a wire held between the toes. But the greater test of Curtis as an actor was the escapologist's inclination towards mysticism, which seemed eventually to be the major force of his compulsion. The film presented him as an exhibitionist, too; and commercial motivation was stressed. The showman's need to maintain his public, for his personal gratification *and* for money, could be accepted as relatively commonplace.

But the courting of danger, and indeed death, would seem to point very sharply to a self-destructive facet in an artist's nature; and self-destruction was the keynote in many of these showbiz films. Aerial acts in circuses had often been grist to the cinema's mill, but in the Fifties there were two examples that brought home the ugliness of the spangled set-up, not for the first time but rather more severely than before.

Trapeze (1956) was a Hollywood film made in Europe by the British director Carol Reed, with location work at the Cirque d'Hiver in Paris. Primarily it was about the persistent efforts of an injured aerialist (Burt Lancaster) to make a comeback; but its one great sequence came as a prelude, showing the acrobat's fall. It began, to the music of "The Blue Danube," as a filmic celebration of man's ability to make the air his element, and it was a heady and exuberant occasion until a sudden misjudgement brought the music to an abrupt halt, followed by a moment of shocked silence and then loud cries of alarm from the crowd as the inert, broken body lay on the sawdust below.

There was a similar incident in Cecil B. DeMille's *The Greatest Show on Earth* (1952), involving Cornel Wilde as an aerialist who competed with Betty Hutton in something like an intoxication of rivalry, each trying to outdo the other. The circus manager (Charlton Heston) had forbidden the aerialist to work without a net below, but the Wilde character severed the ropes of the net and, in a dazzling display of skill, attempted too much and fell to the ground, losing the use of an arm. He remained with the circus in a humbler capacity, loved by the girl who had goaded him. Again the question of motivation was implicit. Cornel Wilde himself summed it up astutely: "The aerialist in the film risks his life all the time, from a kind of com-

(Left) James Stewart, Cornel Wilde, and Charlton Heston in THE GREATEST SHOW ON EARTH. (Right) Ida Lupino, Shelley Winters, Jack Palance in THE BIG KNIFE

pulsion to be in the public eye and to get a thrill from danger—which many people do." There was a duality to the danger-thrill, experienced directly by the aerialist and vicariously by the crowd whose response to the spectacle was pitched ambiguously between the therapeutic tension of seeing somebody else in danger ("Thank God it's not me") and the barbaric pleasures of the Roman arena. *The Greatest Show on Earth* was probably the best of all Cecil B. De-Mille's heavyweight spectaculars: a move into the modern world—and the circus seemed more apt as source material for his talents than the Bible. Charlton Heston had a worthwhile change from Moses and other epic-figures, bringing firm authority to his study of the circus manager, grappling with crises, meeting temperament with tact. He was tough yet sympathetic, because the majority of showbiz films were inclined to favour the boss-men: they were made, after all, under the jurisdiction of boss-men who probably disliked to insult their own breed.

There were exceptions to this, however. A mild case was the Hollywood producer (Kirk Douglas) in *The Bad and the Beautiful* (1952, Vincente Minnelli). Although the character of the producer was ostensibly the bad man of the title, he was disclosed, in varied flashbacks, to be a creature with a certain amount of good in him: fair enough, since good and bad are mingled in everybody. A neat screenplay by Charles Schnee encompassed the flashback recollections of three people who felt they had been exploited by the producer in the past: Lana Turner as a star, incidentally alcoholic of course; Dick Powell as a writer; and Barry Sullivan as a director. Minnelli contrived to moderate the gloss. The three long-sufferers decided to join forces with the producer again at a point of crisis in his career, but this was not presented as a big warm gesture of support for an out-size underdog. Each of the three acknowledged that, for all his ruthlessness, the producer had been of service; despite his unscrupulous streak, they had cause to be grateful for the opportunities and the wealth he had given them.

Much tougher was Robert Aldrich's *The Big Knife* (1955), another film adaptation of a play by Clifford Odets whose hearty dislike for the archetypal bad boss-men of Hollywood was transmitted ferociously through Rod Steiger's performance as a grotesque producer who bent an actor to his will. Jack Palance was in top form as the actor, his ideals long since abandoned in favour of Hollywood affluence, his strength of body and of mind diminished by the machinations of the boss. Aldrich observed the ironic contrast between the actor's luxury in his expensive house, where he was exercised and massaged like a thoroughbred animal, and the pressures that assailed his intelligent mind. Melodrama flared up in the conflict between producer and actor. A rather strenuous touch in the plot was the actor's responsibility for the death of a girl he had knocked down, accidentally, while driving under the influence of drink. The producer had arranged for some lackey at the studio to shoulder the blame and the prison sentence; and this skeleton was hauled forth from the cupboard to be rattled ominously when the actor wanted to break free of Hollywood's debilitating influences and pursue his art on the stage. Reaching a peak in a tremendous confrontation between Steiger and Palance, the film's dramatic tension was reinforced by the heartfelt anger of the writing.

Clifford Odets contributed as well to the screenplay of *Sweet Smell of Success* (1957) in collaboration with Ernest Lehman, and here the object of indignation was a columnist operating around Broadway (Burt Lancaster) and obtaining the dirty low-down on celebrities from a publicist (Tony Curtis): the two actors, uncommonly cast, were quick to seize their offbeat chances and dispense the vitriol; and the cutting edge of the Odets pen was matched by Alexander Mackendrick's direction and the sharp black-and-white cinematography of James Wong Howe on locations similar to those of *Stage Struck*.

By the end of the decade, audiences might well have had their fill of showbiz neurosis. A salutary and entertaining reactionary movie, from the redoubtable George Cukor, was *Heller in Pink Tights* (1959), a joyful reconstruction of the way things were—give or take the concomitant levity—among members of a theatrical troupe in the old American west, touring the settlements from Cheyenne to Virginia City in the days of Wyatt Earp and Jesse James. Engagingly photographed in colour, the film established its ambiance in an opening chase sequence. A wagon carrying "Healy's Dramatic and Concert Company" was pursued by creditors to the Wyoming border, beyond which the thespians were immune. Inside the wagon, Healy (Anthony Quinn) was teaching his star (Sophia Loren) the niceties of Hamlet's speech to the players. Like stars of the Fifties, these itinerant barnstormers of old had found it necessary to maintain an outward show of regality to their public, wherever possible. So nothing of their hair-raising escape from the creditors was evident in their grand manner as they arrived in Cheyenne, a tough town where unfortunate men were tied to dismantled doors and raised up from the ground to serve as targets for bullets. Violence was a day-to-day normality—sex was quite another matter. Certain proprieties had to be observed, according to the Cheyenne theatre manager who discouraged a fragment of Offenbach from Sophia Loren. *La Belle Hélène* would never do for the local public: "You can't get away with making fun out of marriage." So Healy changed the programme. *Mazeppa* was staged instead. Casting aside a cloak, Sophia Loren stood transformed—

improbably—into a man. Furthermore, she was tied to a horse which ran around the stalls of the theatre and back up to the stage where it pranced aboard a treadmill and galloped in an illusion of perpetual motion, the girl still secure upon its back.

New trouble with a creditor, and a loss in a poker game, prompted another hasty journey aboard the wagon, through countryside known to be full of hostile Apaches. When the Indians attacked, Cukor supplied a jaunty variation upon Western traditions. The Apache warriors plucked costumes from the wagon and bedecked themselves in unaccustomed finery: a sprightly storm of feathers gave place to menace when they set the wagon on fire. The sequence was a cunning mixture of frivolity and hardship, culminating in another escape passage as members of the troupe fled on horseback.

The grandest escape of all was saved for the climax. A gunman (Steve Forrest), after an hilarious knockabout fight with Quinn in the wings of a theatre in Bonanza, retreated from villains by substituting himself for the *Mazeppa* actress. Bound to the horse, and heavily disguised, he galloped through the stalls to a roar of applause, but instead of returning to the stage and the treadmill, he rode on, right out of the theatre—and out of town. *Heller in Pink Tights* evoked the birth pangs of American showbiz, in high style; and many a star of the Fifties might have observed it with a trace of envy, for it recalled a period when players had so many urgent problems to overcome that there could scarcely have been time for neurosis to develop.

8. When Shall We Laugh?

HOLLYWOOD SUFFERED a dearth of comedy in the Fifties. One theory about this was based upon the fact that the majority of good comedy writers and performers are inclined to take life seriously; therefore, since times were grim, not only in regard to Hollywood's precarious status but in respect of world politics, a sense of humour no longer came easily to practitioners in what had always been regarded as a very difficult field at the best of times. It was a credible explanation. At the beginning of the decade, for example, virtually carrying over the smart comedy style of the Forties, Vincente Minnelli directed *Father of the Bride* (1950) with a polish that would soon become outmoded.

Spencer Tracy and Joan Bennett were the fairly well-heeled parents caught up in the domestic and diplomatic crises of their daughter's impending wedding. Elizabeth Taylor was the put-upon bride-to-be, growing increasingly edgy under the strain as father saw the guest list increasing, the plans proliferating until the house was no longer his own and at the end there was a gigantic bill to be footed. But when it was over, amid the expensive debris, these parents experienced a species of afterglow. It had been trying, but after all they could afford it. Whereas in 1956 a similar situation in *The Catered Affair* (U.K. title: *Wedding Breakfast*) involved a descent of the social ladder, with Ernest Borgnine as a cab driver living in the Bronx, Bette Davis as the housebound mother who is determined that her child shall have a properly "catered" wedding reception, and Debbie Reynolds as the girl herself (an expert performance, and an earthy departure from her dewy norm) who prefers to elope and avoid the family squabbles. Gore Vidal's screenplay, from a television play by Paddy Chayefsky, was certainly full of wit but even fuller of sad implications about conventional ideas of social status. Bette Davis reined in nicely as a woman who had long since lost the savour of life and had become a scold, automatically manipulating some morsel in a frying pan while uttering rebukes, or giving way to self-pity and brushing her hair at the same time: the essential humdrum matron of small means whose hands perform the routine duties of their own accord, no matter how distracted her emotions. Comedy it remained, to be sure, but with a darker strain that would develop increasingly towards the black satire which typified the mood of the mid-Fifties and extended throughout the Sixties as well.

Where once the cinema public rallied to a series of broad comedies made to a formula, very often shown as second features, television scooped the market with assembly-line series. A moderately amusing movie of 1950, *Francis,* directed by Arthur Lubin, had as its title character a talking mule who conversed with Donald O'Connor. Elementary incongruity: the mule's mouth aided by some adequate cartoon-trickery and a human voice issuing forth. The notion ran to nearly

half a dozen films, which was good going for those days, but it was only a matter of time before audiences realised that humour of this level could be had by their firesides; and, indeed, TV eventually whipped up a breezy little series, *Mister Ed*, about a talking horse. Some of the comic stars found their future incomes in TV as well. One of the most successful shifts in the direction of the small screen was made by Lucille Ball, who was already enjoying the TV-fruits of *I Love Lucy* when she made a fleeting but hilarious return to cinema in Minnelli's *The Long, Long Trailer* (1953). Partnered by Desi Arnaz, as on TV, she did her familiar clowning in circumstances ideally suited to her zany persona, so expertly cultivated and sustained. The plot was a mere excuse for a string of gags, visual and verbal, as the pair took a honeymoon tour in their trailer, a confined space conducive to all manner of muddle. The trailer, in effect, became a super-symbol of the inanimate objects which beset humanity—and the Lucille Ball humanity was accident prone, of course, as the wretched vehicle subjected her to one indignity after another. Yet, even with the scenic values of the trip, and the broader and broader expertise of Minnelli, a roll in the cinema aisle was not necessarily better than a roll on the drawing room floor.

In the circumstances, it was ironically apt for a Hollywood comedy of 1952 to be entitled *Singin' in the Rain*. Putting up a brave and breezy show at a time when both comedies and musicals were starting to feel the strain, this one proved a happy joke to set beside the downbeat splendours of *Sunset Boulevard*. Directed by Gene Kelly and Stanley Donen, it made game of the painful transition from silent movies to sound in the late Twenties, the era when its title song was new. Primarily a musical, this was very much a comedy as well. The screenplay by Adolph Green and Betty Comden, brimful of merriment, had Gene Kelly as a guy who played mood music on a violin to help the silent stars emote while directors shouted exhortations. The violinist, Don, made progress. First, as a stunt man, he survived crashes in planes, motor-cycle rides over clifftops into water far below, and explosions at close range; and soon he was co-starring with a glamour

*Opposite: similar situations at different social
levels—FATHER OF THE BRIDE (above) and THE
CATERED AFFAIR (below)*

queen (Jean Hagen) whose charm was prodigious while movies remained mute but whose voice couldn't meet the challenge of talkies, which gave the heroine, Kathy (Debbie Reynolds), her big chance. She dubbed the voice, and, when the glamour queen took a bow after the premiere and was called upon to sing in person, the humble Kathy stood behind the curtain and sang for her, until Don and his pal Cosmo (Donald O'Connor) whipped the curtain away to foil the tiresome star and make their beloved Kathy an overnight sensation. This prankish stuff was just slightly softened by Kelly's famous song and dance solo to the title tune, puddle paddling, twirling on a lamp-post, holding his umbrella unopened and exulting in the downpour until a passing cop eyed him suspiciously, bringing his elated mood down to earth. Donald O'Connor did an excellent knockabout number called "Make 'Em

Gene Kelly as a former stunt man, elevated to the perils of stardom at the end of the silent era, in SINGIN' IN THE RAIN

Laugh," singing through pratfalls and climbing up walls, as well as delivering a sprightly parody on the speech exercises that twisted the tongues of silent stars to make them soundtrack-worthy—"Moses supposes his toeses are roses, but Moses supposes erroneously. . . ."

In fact, the word had taken over to so great an extent in Hollywood comedies of the post-silent decades that writers of amusing dialogue, at various brow-levels, were much in demand in the Fifties. Since they were no longer thick on the ground, George Cukor might well have counted himself among the luckiest of directors because he was blessed with the inextinguishable mirth that flowed from the minds of Garson Kanin and his actress-wife Ruth Gordon. The collusion between this gifted pair and a director as good as Cukor, as well as the astute comedy acting of Judy Holliday, yielded a crop so agreeable that you would wonder just why there was so much gloom about. Indeed, in this chapter especially, the temptation to dwell upon the choicest movies, which are inevitably the most interesting, makes it obligatory to emphasise again that work of this quality was uncommon—increasingly so as the decade wore on. In 1950, however, Cukor was in clover with *Born Yesterday,* a safe and simple film version of Kanin's hit play in which Judy Holliday repeated her stage triumph as the prototype dumb blonde, mistress of an uncouth oaf (Broderick Crawford) who had made his pile as a junk dealer and could afford to keep her in luxury and employ a journalist (William Holden) to educate her. The interplay between this trio was joyful stuff. Cukor kept his camera still in acknowledgement of Judy Holliday's power to hold the eye as she repeatedly bested Crawford at gin rummy, although he denied it: the quiet blank-faced assurance of the girl, the riffling of the cards in her deliberate hands, reduced her opponent to a jelly of nervous frustration. But this was adopted theatre, aptly planed down for cinema. *The Marrying Kind* (1951) was considerably more. Not quite so dumb a blonde on this occasion, Judy Holliday as Florence was resolved to do a half-hour's "thinking" each day on her own account. The screenplay by Kanin and Ruth Gordon was framed by a consultation in the office of a sympathetic but practical female judge: Florence and her husband (Aldo Ray) are contemplating divorce. The judge ferrets around smoothly for the reasons: "What is it that makes you incompatible?" "Being married to each other," says Florence. But clearly it is not so elementary. Aldo Ray's gravel-voice had issued from the mouth of

173

"What is it that makes you incompatible?" "Being married to each other."—Judy Holliday, Aldo Ray, Madge Kennedy in THE MARRYING KIND

Judy Holliday as he recounted to the judge how they first met in New York's Central Park, the words they exchanged, the fairly easy pick-up that led to married life in a modest apartment. Flashbacks, prompted by the judge's questions, bring amusing revelations of two simple but hopeful minds. The husband has a job in the postal department, and dreams of better things. He has a nightmare, as well, beautifully filmic in its glide from realism to fantasy. There lies Aldo Ray on his back, snoring but with eyes wide open as he begins to drift strangely downward, in a supine position, towards the foot of the bed which becomes a conveyor belt on which he is carried like some postal package and hurtled down a shoot to emerge in his place of work. The dream is a recall of anxiety. He is due to meet Florence and accompany her to a party. Yet he must clear the floor of scattered ball-bearings first, an imposition fraught with slapstick indignities from which he emerges without his trousers, racing through the busy night-streets in jacket and underpants, backgrounded by realistic neon-lit Manhattan, while before him in multiple images stands Florence in the uniform of a policeman, aiming a gun in his direction and firing. Waking life is less fantasticated. An extraordinary shock effect comes in a later episode on a sunlit day after a picnic meal with their small son. Cukor holds a medium close shot of Judy Holliday, strumming a ukelele and singing "Dolores," while gradually we become aware of people moving behind her, legs passing in the background faster and faster until we know that something is seriously wrong. And at last the sustained image of the singing face is replaced by a shot of many people crowding to the edge of a lake—and now she learns that her son has been drowned. Not suddenly, but swiftly, and with a certainty of spectator-control that would not be matched again in Hollywood cinema until Billy Wilder filmed *The Apartment* (1960), Cukor made a tremendous switch from merriment to drama. At the end of this singular episode, the return to the linking scene in the judge's office was in quite a different vein from all that had gone before: a valid transition, of course, since life can be funny or pleasant one minute and deflating the next. At the same time, while the method of beginning a romantic film in terms of comedy and then gravitating steadily towards serious treatment was by no means new, the particular darkness here was a prefiguration of the darker mood that dominated the best of American cinema in the Fifties, marking a departure from rosy escapism.

For Cukor the decade began well and continued tolerably, give or take such glum spots as *Bhowani Junction* (1955) and *Les Girls* (1957). He cleaved a good deal to comedy films at this period of his career. The Kanins, having given him a superb screenplay for the agreeable Katharine Hepburn-Spencer Tracy partnership in the 1949 jollities of *Adam's Rib,* did very nearly as well again with the same stars matching their wit to the amiable light clowning of Aldo Ray as a dim-brained pugilist in *Pat and Mike* (1952). The following year Cukor dealt in the charm of Ruth Gordon's *The Actress* and then in the astringent satire of *It Should Happen to You,* with the two Kanins pitching in again and Judy Holliday doing her dumb blonde bit (eventually, but not yet, she became stuck in this rut, which was a pity).

(Left) Bob Hope as SON OF PALEFACE. (Right) Louis Armstrong—"We were taught right from Beethoven and Bach"

Serving also to introduce Jack Lemmon to cinema audiences, *It Should Happen to You* (1953) was a putdown of the gullible. The blonde and daffy Gladys Glover thought how nice it would be to see her name on billboards around New York, just like a celebrated star. So she paid to have it put there: just the name—Gladys Glover. Nobody had ever heard of her before, but the impact was enough to arouse curiosity and bring her lucrative offers from the wide-eyed denizens of advertising and showbiz: never mind about talent, the girl had that valuable commodity—"a NAME."

Names that had been earned the hard way, especially the stars who specialised in fun, had their ups and depressing downs as the public's corporate sense of humour became harder to assess. Bob Hope seemed quite as side-splitting as ever, so long as he was cast in reminiscent movies. *My Favourite Spy* (1951, Norman Z. McLeod) employed much the same recipe of thriller-spoofing with a glamour girl titillating Hope (in this case Hedy Lamarr) as had been dished up satisfactorily in *My Favourite Blonde* (1942) and *My Favourite Brunette* (1947). Likewise, a hit of 1948, *The Paleface* was paralleled happily by *Son of Paleface* (1952), all the better for being directed by the sprightly Frank Tashlin who also had a hand in the screenplay, giving Hope the kind of lines he could get away with nimbly: "Dad's head wasn't empty. I know 'cause Mother used to rattle it for me when I was a baby." Same set-up: nature's coward trying to brave it out in the Wild West. Same hit song, "Buttons and Bows" with rejigged lyrics. Same wonderfully incongruous leading lady: Jane Russell, this time as a female bandit who also runs the Dirty Shame Saloon in Sawbuck Pass. It could hardly go wrong, and it didn't. Evidently the not-quite-lowest-denominator hadn't varied much between 1948 and 1952. On the other hand, the "Road" series, teaming Hope with Bing Crosby and Dorothy Lamour, had brisked along cheerily from their very start in 1940 but when the sixth of them showed up in 1952, *Road to Bali* (Hal Walker), traces of exhaustion had set in. A pity—especially since the writing credits included the name of Frank Butler, familiar from the early ones, including the very best of the whole lot, *Road to Morocco* (1942). A good gag near the start of the *Bali* jaunt had Hope and Crosby launching into the familiar song about "lambs who have lost their way" and an insert of genuine sheep to provide the "Baa-baa-baa": alas, as the reels unwound, it seemed all too appropriate. Only comparatively, perhaps. Previous *Roads* had led to funnier events. A congenial touch was the persona invented for Dorothy Lamour, the "palpitating princess" Lalah McTavish, offspring of an island beauty and a kilted traveller whose life-size portraits dominated the palace hallway. For Hope, so needful of gags, so adroit in his timing of them, material proved thin in the Fifties, although his show-personality, which he seemed to switch on like a light when "action" was called, kept him afloat through waters that were sometimes downright sluggish: certainly in the Venetian capers of *Casanova's Big Night* (1954, Norman Z. McLeod), and the sentimental drool of *The Seven Little Foys* (1955, Melville Shavelson) which required him to personify a famous old-time vaudeville comic, Eddie Foy, to the glory of neither of them.

Danny Kaye had some luckless assignments, too, after his sparkling start in the Forties. As *Hans Christian Andersen* (1952, Charles Vidor) he pronounced Copenhagen with a broad "a" but eased without too much difficulty through a cute little song called "Ugly Duckling" and was able to revert to the jubilantly manic style that suited him best in "The King's New Clothes": the idea of applying Frank Loesser's brand of song to the Andersen fairy tales had an offbeat charm in spots; and the film was popular at a time when Hollywood still had reason to believe in the validity of such a concept as "family entertainment." (It would be a very odd family in which seniors and juniors had the same tastes; but the idea of getting them all to the cinema together could work if the denominator were sufficiently low.) Kaye drew his public, to be sure, although he reached a bit far in *Me and the Colonel* (1957, Peter Glenville) as the eternally disorientated Jew, trying to flee Paris just before the Nazi occupation. One can understand how this serio-comic subject, from S. N. Behrman's play *Jacobowsky and the Colonel* based on Franz Werfel's original, would have appealed to Kaye, and it was certainly a brave try. Far easier, and more popular, but sloppy in the extreme was *The Five Pennies* (1959, Melville Shavelson) with Kaye as Red Nichols, the jazz man of the Twenties, hot on cornet but, as depicted, a bit of a bore. Things brightened notably when Louis Armstrong got into the act and Kaye joined him in a scat rendition of "When the Saints Go Marching In." Armstrong could rescue anything, of course: he even managed to justify the plot-intrusion of a jazz festival upon the musicalised 1956 version of *The Philadelphia Story,* which was called *High Society* and was all right in its way, decently directed by Charles Walters and nicely provided with Cole Porter numbers, but putting Grace Kelly and Bing Crosby and Frank Sinatra in the unfortunate predicament of demonstrating all too clearly that Katharine Hepburn and Cary Grant and James Stewart had been much nearer the mark when they played the same roles without musical interruptions in Cukor's movie of 1940.

Nevertheless the Louis Armstrong contributions to both *The Five Pennies* and *High Society* had a significance in the "rock 'n' rolling" second half of the Fifties. They perpetuated jazz. In Armstrong's view, at the end of the decade, "Jazz has so much to say, so much to teach the youngsters. They have nothing to derive from this new music they've got. Jujitsu music, I call it. Progressive and modern! What's the youngster going to learn from that but . . tear his lip up? We were taught right from Beethoven and Bach . . Liszt . . beautiful things. And for funerals we played beautiful marches going to the cemetery, and 'When the Saints Go Marching In' coming back from the cemetery. The youngsters can't get that experience nowadays because there's nobody to tell it to them but the old-timers. And the one that listens always turns out to be a good musician, I don't care what he plays. When I was a kid I never wanted to put the trumpet down, and I still don't. And I still feel as strong as I did when I was a lad of twenty as far as the trumpet's concerned"—he was about sixty at the time—"If you take care of your system, you can do a lot of things. I think one should, because once you're dead you ain't coming back. You might as well stay as long as you can, and feel good at the same time. Why live on earth feeling bad all the time?"

It was a pertinent question. Hollywood vagaries in the matter of comedy had been one reflection of the prevalent uncertainty. Jazz, as culture and as joy, was a hardy perennial. The throwback comedies had fitful pleasures to offer. Like Bob Hope, Danny Kaye was at his funniest in the Fifties when he did what he had been doing most notably in the Forties. The best Kaye movie of the decade, in my view, was *The Court Jester* (1955), especially when the climax threw him into verbal complexities; his special and brilliant gift, his way with tongue-twiddling words, was marvellously endowed in a dialogue he shared with Mildred Natwick, she as a medieval sorceress, he as the wary participant in a joust who would just as soon eliminate his antagonist before the event with knockout drops in the wine. Hence he reiterates, in confused sequence, the knowledge imparted by the sorceress: "The pellet with the poison's in the vessel with the pestle, the chalice from the palace has the brew that is true" until the increasingly muddled situation is carried to the point of delirium by the introduction of a "flagon" embossed with the image of a "dragon." The permutations are bewildering and blissful. One could think of similar plights: not least the dilemma of Eddie Cantor in *Roman Scandals* (1933, Frank Tuttle), holding two pies, one lethal the other not, and repeating *sotto voce*, "The one without the parsley is the one without the poison" until he discovers to his horror that somebody has put parsley on both. Hardly anything is new, but old gags can be refreshed, which is really the reason *The Court Jester* held such joyous and corny sway. Credits for direction and screenplay were shared equally by Norman Panama and

179

Melvin Frank, who perpetuated a venerable brand of hokum with finesse.

Hollywood toyed occasionally with a stylised form, mainly by the use of sets that were deliberately artificial, as in the musicals *Red Garters* (1953) and *Li'l Abner* (1959). Both were underestimated. Many people dismissed them as being "stagey," failing to take the point that such was their intent. George Marshall, a resilient Hollywood veteran, must surely have enjoyed taking the mickey out of the Western at a time when the *genre* was beginning to grow quite serious. Certainly there was more virtue to be found in the new trend of psychological Westerns than in such a harmless lark as *Red Garters,* but the balance of things would be awry if there were not still room for a joke. Indeed, the reluctance or inability of many to see the joke was a sorry reflection of the general state of mind. Nothing could have been much funnier, at the time, than the elegance of the Western hero (pop singer Guy Mitchell) dressed all in white and riding a white horse to confront a black-clad-and-horse-to-match villain (Gene Barry). The saloon girl (Rosemary Clooney) did her stuff against a *décor* of primitive red. The main street of town, beneath a buttercup sky, was palpably fragile, its buildings mere façades with no architectural substance. And what went on was a romp. Hardly as good a fun-Western, really, as Marshall's 1939 diversion *Destry Rides Again,* but imbued with a healthy spirit of satire nevertheless, and prefiguring the stylised look of *Li'l Abner,* which Norman Panama and Melvin Frank adapted from their Broadway script, based on the famous cartoon strip by Al Capp, with some good lowdown lyrics by Johnny Mercer. Stubby Kaye as Marryin' Sam walked the central square of Dogpatch as an actor might tread the boards, and the setting as equally histrionic, dominated by the statue of the town's founder, Jubilation T. Cornpone (who, after a night with a femme fatale, had become "old weary-and-worn-pone"). Against manifestly painted backdrops, the hillbillies celebrated Sadie Hawkins Day (an annual occasion for the girls to chase and catch the men); and the human performers, under Melvin Frank's direction, maintained a delirious identification with their comic-strip prototypes: especially Peter Palmer's sturdy but gormless Abner and Julie Newmar's embodiment (the only word) of the glamorous Stupefyin' Jones.

It was customary, however, to "rationalise" most of the stylised movies by presenting them as dreams or even nightmares, as in the near-expressionist castle where hundreds of little boys were seated to play upon a monstrously long and curving piano with endless keyboards at two levels to accommodate them: their harassed hands provided *The Five Thousand Fingers of Dr. T.* (1953, Roy Rowland). *Dr. T.* himself, a slave-driving piano-teacher with a penchant for ostentatious attire (Hans Conreid), was a creation of the offbeat cartoonist "Dr. Seuss," who also scripted UPA's animated cartoon *Gerald McBoing Boing* (who "couldn't speak words—he went *boing boing* instead"). Both these instances, with children as central figures, showed a leaning towards the black comedy vein so typical of the era.

In fact, with *Gerald McBoing Boing* (1951, directed by Robert Cannon) and another one-reel cartoon from James Thurber's *Unicorn in the Garden* (1953), the UPA group developed a style far enough removed from the traditional animated shorts to encompass a virtually abstract treatment, narrated by James Mason, of Edgar Allan Poe's *The Tell-Tale Heart* (also 1953, directed by Ted Parmalee). The serious cartoon did not become a vogue, however, and UPA made its strongest appeal with a series about a myopic middle-class American, *Mr. Magoo,* who drew incorrect assumptions in every situation, occasionally at danger to his life but with never a qualm: the symbolic put-down of the hidebound attitude was emphasised by a splendidly bumbling voice (Jim Backus). UPA (United Productions of America) was formed by an ex-Disney artist, Stephen Bosustow, during the latter half of the Forties. Others joined him, including Leo Salkin who had worked on the Siamese Cat sequence of Disney's feature-length cartoon *Lady and the Tramp* (1955) and who expressed the view that Disney was "one of the greatest story-tellers in and out of the cartoon medium. The difference between Disney's approach and the UPA approach is that the Disney studio is by and large an extension of Walt's thinking whereas UPA allows its directors to work pretty much as *they* see a subject. We got away from the cute little round figures that Disney has done so skilfully and we began to work for a form that we felt was an honest cartoon shape—a flat figure with a flat background." This kind of line drawing was stylised, frankly disassociated from the naturalistic effects of depth in landscaping, snowfalls and sunsets, that frequently lured the spectator into accepting the horrific or sentimental passages of Disney films as real within their own fantasy world. By eschewing naturalism, Salkin felt that UPA could "deal more with the problems of human beings, rather than of bunny rabbits and dogs and cats and mice. The cartoon can probe many serious questions, but it does this best with humour, with a lightness of touch." Indeed, Disney's artists did this very thing, using rather flat figures to represent humans, in *Man in Space* (1956), virtually a documentary about the technical and biological aspects of space exploration, meticulously detailed but presented with a sense of humour.

Yet there was still a big market for the established Disney mode of animated story-telling, Americanised from durable material. His full-length cartoons, *Peter Pan* (1952) and *The Sleeping Beauty* (1958) were stardusty and sugary, with the customary dash of violence which bothered adults more than children, and with variable lardings of song: a nicely wishful number called "The Second Star to the Right" guided the flying children in *Peter Pan*, but a ghastly lyric was shackled to Tchaikovsky's garland waltz when the post-dormant belle and her reviver shared memories of a previous meeting "Once upon a Dream." The Disney studios launched into non-animated movies as well, none of more than commercial consequence except for *Old Yeller* (1957, directed by Robert Stevenson), set in the hill country of Texas *circa* 1860, and using a deal of violence in quite a viable way to illustrate the point that life must go on despite vicissitudes: "A man can't afford to waste all the good part of his life worrying about the bad part," said a father to a son whose brave pet dog had been stricken with rabies. It was the child who fired the shot to put the poor beast out of its misery; and, although a certain amount of comedy alleviated the anguish, and a puppy afforded consolation at the end, the homespun philosophy was surprisingly firm. Disney branched out in another direction with some nature study films, of which the best was *The Living Desert* (1953). The vast desert areas of the south-western U.S.A. were explored by colour cameras. Violence in animal behaviour was juxtaposed with the splendours of nature. Time-lapse photography caused a flower to bud and bloom swiftly, and clouds to race across a spacious sky. And, in fact, the stylisation was more progressive than in Disney's cartoons. A mating ritual between two scorpions was repeat-edited and timed to the exhortations of a square-dance "caller" in a technically stunning little sequence. In Disney's domain it was considered unwise to keep faces straightened for too long at a stretch.

The UPA group, however, provided cartoon links both merry and grim for Stanley Kramer's production of *The Fourposter* (1952, directed by Irving Reis), from a play by Jan De Hartog with a cast of two: a taxing affair in cinema, of course, played with considerable distinction by Rex Harrison and Lilli Palmer. It was the story of a marriage, beginning in New York at the turn of the century, the bride and groom young and optimistic in their attic room with its one grand item of furniture, a fourposter bed. Their circumstances altered: they changed as their environment changed, but the fourposter remained with them, and the cartoon interludes bridged the passages of time with proliferating line drawings of the city growing denser around the house in which they lived, of the grim horrors of the First World War in which their son was killed, and of the Twenties with gangsters and speakeasies and flying machines. This was also a movie which gravitated cunningly from initial comedy to despair and an ultimate pathos, nicely sustained by the two players in one of the cinema's most sentimental and yet most credible portrayals of old age.

Another, and funnier, sample of the two-hander (alleviated at the beginning by a delightful performance by Robert Morley as a missionary) was John Huston's *The African Queen* (1951), taken from C. S. Forester's novel and filmed in British studios and on African locations. For the greater part of the film, the screen was held by Katharine Hepburn as the missionary's sister, a formidable spinster, and Humphrey Bogart as a sinful rough diamond. Their adventures aboard a small boat during the First World War afforded plenty of action, but, even so, it was unusual to see how well the attention could be maintained by only two players. Of course, they were experts, gaining numerous laughs and frequent compassion as well in their bickering, their hardships, and their eventual rapport. The sight of Bogart plucking leeches from his chest in shuddery revulsion was as telling a human touch as any of the shrewd gradations Katharine Hepburn gave to the woman's thaw. But the trick was not to be equalled by Huston in 1956, when he was stranded with a lesser subject, *Heaven Knows, Mr. Allison*: the Second World War this time; Deborah Kerr as a nun was confined to a desert island with Robert Mitchum as a beefy marine, and there really wasn't very much that either God or Huston could do for them.

An interesting comedy partnership that struggled through the early years of the Fifties before dissolving was that of Dean Martin and

*Before the partnership dissolved—Jerry Lewis and
Dean Martin in SCARED STIFF*

Jerry Lewis, who had been filming as a team since the end of the
Forties. The best of their fitful vehicles was *Scared Stiff* (1952, George
Marshall), landing them, after a long preamble, among the mock-
terrors of a haunted island. For Lewis, this was ideal territory; but
his individual brand of humour was so sufficient unto itself that he
never seemed to need a "feed" and therefore Martin was a superfluous
figure, singing the occasional song but looking as if he might do better
on his own—as indeed they both did before the decade was over.
Scared Stiff, incidentally, was a re-make of a Bob Hope movie of 1940,
The Ghost Breakers, and a major twist of plot in both these films, in
which organ music yielded the key to a mystery, was also used in
Murder, He Says (1945): all three films were directed by Marshall,
obviously a man to get full value from a gag—it was equally funny
each time.

Of course, the supernatural always fared better with audiences when couched in comedy. A serious fantasy like Don Siegel's *Invasion of the Body Snatchers* (1956), filled with darkling intimations of alien powers, draining away the mind of the individual, reducing humans to blank subservience, was so unnervingly credible in a world of scientific advance and political fear as to induce a protective reaction in many. "Just another science fiction thriller" to the greater part of its public, although the brave looked deeper and saw much more. The same was true of Byron Haskin's *The War of the Worlds* (1953), with a screenplay by Barré Lyndon based on the H. G. Wells hair-raiser, transferred to California, where the humble merriment of a square dance was cut short by an electricity failure, quickly attributed to Martians who had landed in what had been considered a dangerous meteor but was in fact a spacecraft more sophisticated than anything known to earthlings. The ingenious George Pal, formerly occupied in Hollywood on comic shorts made with puppets, became a space-movie pioneer in the Fifties, and this Martian contraption was a testament to his skill: he produced the movie as well. From the spacecraft rose a sort of periscope, like a cobra's head, seeing and demolishing, surrounded at times by an electro-magnetic "blister" that made it impervious to the most deadly of man's weapons. While focussed upon one little area of the U.S.A., the story embraced the entire earth as news of other landings began to seep through from major capitals until communication systems failed, signifying Martian victory. The world had been rendered impotent. Annihilation was near. Washington heads were spinning; but the news-vendors, for as long as they could, just thrived on it—in a superb little fragment of irony, a taciturn old lady sat beside her stack of newspapers on a frenzied sidewalk, crying "Read all about the Martian invasion—they're in New York and Miami—fighting outside L.A.—*aaaaaaawll* about it!!" Admittedly, a humdrum hero and heroine dragged the *genre* back into second gear, and there was one tiresome passage where, on the verge of starvation, they found and fried some eggs and then let the tempting things go cold while they prattled on with their dialogue. But, with atomic defence proving futile, and a clergyman with crucifix upheld approaching the Martian's magic circle and perishing, thereby eradicating any sympathy that might have been given to his policy of "try to communicate with them first, and shoot later if you have to," the gigantic metaphor was all too clear. The uptight political climate, the obvious association of the Martian junta with the Communist threat to democracy, wiped the smirk from cynical faces in the darkness of cinemas, but the tendency was to emerge with the consoling thought of fantasy foremost, and Hollywood marketed *The War of the Worlds* as an entertainment.

Even the timelessly restive legend of Faust was turned to farce, and was indeed entertaining if a bit glacial, in *Damn Yankees!* (1958), directed by George Abbott and Stanley Donen from the Broadway musical of the same name (the movie's U.K. title was *What Lola Wants*). From the New York cast, Gwen Verdon as Lola, a witch in showgirl trappings, and Ray Walston as Applegate, a dapper and somewhat dithery Mephistopheles, played hell with the soul of a middle-aged baseball enthusiast, granting his wish to be young and to participate. Away with the warm lamplight of a conventional home, and on with the smoke-laden night club mist of seductive dreams, together with some orthodox athletic activity in the baseball stadium where a pep-talk was delivered in marvellously corny song ("All you really need is *heart*") and dust was literally raised by a ballplayers ballet on authentic earth. Bob Fosse choreographed delightfully; and Tab Hunter took every advantage of his best Hollywood opportunity as the muscled metamorphosis of the bewitched hero, although nobody quite got the measure of pathos that was needed for the potentially touching little moment when the melancholy "youngster" goes home unrecognised and asks his middle-aged wife if she can rent him a room.

Musicals, however, were considered to be a decreasingly viable proposition in the Fifties. For the foreign markets, the lyrics of songs had always been a bugbear to subtitlers and consequently much of the impact was lost on audiences who didn't know the language; and, of course, musicals were expensive to produce. At the same time, paradoxically, the musical dogdays were by no means dominated by the prevalent security trend of taking up a show that had done well on Broadway. *High Society,* while based on a straight play, was musicalised by Hollywood; likewise *Gigi* (1958, Vincente Minnelli below par, but popular). And *Seven Brides for Seven Brothers* (1954, Stanley Donen; virile choreography from Michael Kidd) was a thoroughgoing original film musical, based loosely on Plutarch by way of the Stephen Vincent Benet story *Sobbin' Women,* a dirty joke somewhat laundered but raunchy enough for most: the "family" audience was still a mite in

Hollywood's eye, and girls who were kidnapped, however willingly, by boys from the backwoods, were not to be raped (exactly) like their Plutarchian predecessors, and had to be wed (eventually).

There were other enterprising attempts, mostly successful, to create musicals exclusively for the screen. One of the very best was *Calamity Jane* (1953, David Butler), especially in its earlier phase before Doris Day, in the title role, shed her buckskin and put down her gun to win the love of Wild Bill Hickok with mooney domesticity. The healthy look, all freckled and fresh-airey, made Doris Day a pushover as Jane, because her acting talent was quite equal to the lowdown humour of such a song as "I Just Blew in from the Windy City." In fact, with musicals on the wane, nobody was quicker than Doris Day to apply survival tactics. Perkily she switched into a non-singing thriller phase, doing very well as the hounded *Julie* (1956, directed and written by

Despite her inexperience in such matters, Doris Day as JULIE was obliged to land a big aircraft when the pilot had been shot

Andrew L. Stone, a great one for carrying suspense to plausible extremities). The put-upon Julie was not a girl to get her coiffure too disturbed by physical and mental stress, but she went through the mill fast enough to forestall the improper guffaw. Her problem, common to various glamour girls over the years, was the perpetual war of nerves waged against her by a mad husband (in this case Louis Jourdan, looking as if he enjoyed the change from his light romantic norm); and there was a sweaty-palmed climax in which the resilient Julie had to take over the pilot's job in a big aircraft and bring it down safely despite her inexperience in such matters. Even better, needless to say, was Hitchcock's application of his mysterious Svengali influence to Doris Day's hysteria about the kidnapping of her little son in *The Man Who Knew Too Much,* made in the very same year. What the suspense master had done for Joan Fontaine and Grace Kelly, to name but a couple of his blondes in lucrative distress, was less remarkable but still a decided progression for a performer as nimble as Doris Day, who leaped in yet another direction in 1959 with *Pillow Talk* (Michael Gordon), the first of what was to become a fitful succession of timorously sexy and intermittently vulgar comedies, several of them uproariously good. This initial scamper proved to be rather superior at the tail end of a decade fraught with a dearth of mirth. To the Gratianos of the era, asking "When shall we laugh, say when?" of a Hollywood whose sense of humour was lapsing, *Pillow Talk* responded with a hearty "Now." It put Doris Day as an interior decorator into paroxysms of frustration at the telephone, because her party line was occupied eternally by the other party (Rock Hudson) singing the same seductive song to the many women in his active love life. Knowing one another only by ear, having exchanged verbal insult whenever she broke in on his chatting and singing, they met eventually, neither knowing the other's identity but each liking what they saw. The man grew wise to the position quickly, leading the woman a merry and spicey dance until she discovered the truth and paid him back by re-decorating his apartment in the style of a sheik's harem, not unlike the kind of pad that would be favoured by affluent hippies ten years later.

At the sloppier end of the social ladder, mirthful in the mire, were the denizens of *God's Little Acre* (1957, Anthony Mann). Robert Ryan played gamely as the superficially religious farmer in Georgia, who didn't furrow his fields but dug big holes in them, year after year, in a futile search for gold. Before the moral at the end, when he came to realise that it was better to grow crops and make a living the hard way, a lot of lust was set before the goggle-eyed spectator, the best and funniest of it taking place between voluptuous Tina Louise and doormat-chested Aldo Ray as a couple of small-brained but full-bodied types, each with a penchant for sex with somebody other than the familiar wedded mate. This was daring stuff in its day, especially since the sleazy setting and the evocation of depression years brought a basic realism to the knockabout humour. The novel of the same name by Erskine Caldwell had been published long before, in the Thirties, but in Hollywood terms the film was ahead of its time. It did make a novel and chirpy departure for Anthony Mann, whose films of the Fifties were otherwise concerned with the war and the old West and a sentimental but agreeable account of *The Glenn Miller Story* (1954, with James Stewart in the title role, and doodle-bug explosions to be incorporated in the rhythm of an outdoor wartime rendition of Miller's signature tune, "In the Mood").

Established directors like Mann were expected to be journeymen. They were often apparently reconciled to this, and probably didn't think of their work as lowly. Howard Hawks, for example, an even more seasoned veteran with some notable films to his credit over the years, was often given assignments that called for nothing greater than competence, and sometimes even that was not enough to save a sticky day: his ludicrous *Land of the Pharaohs* (1955), deploying slaves in extravagant quantity to build a pyramid fit for the biggest possible screen, was a glum example of historical Hollywood tosh, and authentic Egyptian locations couldn't make it look otherwise. Yet Hawks, always at his brightest when comedy was intentional, made a couple of the decade's happier movies, *Monkey Business* (1952) and *Gentlemen Prefer Blondes* (1953). In the first of these, scripted by Ben Hecht and Charles Lederer and I. A. L. Diamond from a Harry Segall story, rejuvenation played riot with the life of a doctor (Cary Grant) who experimented in quest of a potion to boost the vitality of those who had reached their middle years or even gone beyond them. When a chimpanzee escaped and meddled with the ingredients in the doctor's absence, Grant and other members of the cast drank quantities of the monkey brew, mistaking it for water. Old boys played young tricks, especially on Marilyn Monroe, and several reverted to childhood antics while retaining their outward show of maturity. This was a constant belly-laugh. *Gentlemen Prefer Blondes* was comparatively sophisticated, no brasher than it should have been, and bouncing with glee. It had an interesting balance of star power. As a wide-eyed but wily blonde, Lorelei Lee, dedicated to the proposition that "Diamonds Are a Girl's Best Friend," Marilyn Monroe intensified her established image, while Jane Russell's cool and tall Dorothy was neither a foil nor a competitor but a well-chosen partner in this two-girl show, where males were perpetually hoodwinked by the gold-diggers and only one scene was stolen —by a small boy, played by George Winslow, who was given a superb deadpan line in appreciation of Lorelei's "animal magnetism." The plentiful songs were helpful, and Hawks sustained a brisk touch of caricature throughout, culminating in a wacky courtroom scene with Jane Russell in a blonde wig pretending, helpfully and hilariously, to be Marilyn Monroe. The whole thing seemed fresh and filmic, which says a deal for the Hawks flair with comedy because the screenplay was adapted from a stage show based on a novel written in the Twenties by Anita Loos.

The late Twenties, when prohibition and gangsters and jazz conjoined on the threshold of economic chaos, were recalled satirically (in the broadest sense of the term) by Billy Wilder's *Some Like It Hot* (1959). Here we had another star-impersonation: Tony Curtis emulating the Cary Grant voice in an amusing seduction jape with Marilyn Monroe. Female impersonation, too—indeed, this was the long-maintained hit of the show—with both Curtis and Jack Lemmon posing as musicians in an all-girl band, so as to escape the attention of the hoods who had orders to gun them down, because they had both been innocent witnesses of a gangland massacre. It was the kind of situation that might have triggered off a Bob Hope burlesque; but Wilder had something more progressive in mind, and he certainly progressed with it, right up to the point where Joe E. Brown proposed marriage to Jack Lemmon and was not in the least fazed to learn that his bride-to-be was a male in disguise—"Nobody's perfect," said Brown, whizzing his captive away in a speedboat named permissive society, and heading in a direction that film-makers would follow through the years ahead.

Billy Wilder had a good decade, with only minor lapses of form in *Sabrina* (1954) and *Love in the Afternoon* (1957): these required a light romantic touch, which came readily enough to Audrey Hepburn who starred in both of them, but Wilder's way had always been to hit a bit harder. This he did splendidly in most of his Fifties movies, and especially in his bracing version of Agatha Christie's play *Witness for the Prosecution* (1958). In the theatre it had been played straight, but Wilder managed to whoop it up delightfully, going against the grain like a high-powered mower on a recalcitrant lawn, levelling all before him—even Charles Laughton as a sick barrister who refused to lie down but thrived and smirked and leered his way through a maze of mystery and a ripe courtroom climax with a triple-twist ending. The play had been quite popular, so many spectators must have known all the secrets in advance, but Wilder's comical tactics gave melodrama such a lift as to keep us agog, not wondering what would happen so much as what pranks the actors would be required to play. Tyrone Power did handsomely as the smooth rogue who appealed to older women and made the most of it. Marlene Dietrich gave a trick performance, so droll that I must really pay her (and Wilder and Agatha Christie) the compliment of not disclosing its preposterous secret in case there is still somebody somewhere who doesn't know it and might enjoy the surprise when they catch a revival of the film. It has been much revived, and televised, having become something of a classic. Wilder ventured upon Hitchcock territory here, in effect; but he preserved a panache all his own. Hitchcock would probably have been more delicate about it, if he had ever broached this specific thriller, yet the controlled breadth of the Wilder style was brilliantly suited to a plot of such outrageous logic.

Delicacy is not the first word that springs to mind in respect of Hitchcock, of course, but it is certainly the fourth or fifth. It was charmingly evident in that lightest of dark comedies, a paradoxical *soufflé* among essays in the macabre, *The Trouble with Harry* (1956). Adapted from a novel by Jack Trevor Storey, it concerned a corpse discovered in the woods of Vermont. This was Harry, as tiresome when dead as he had been while he was alive. The body was buried to avoid embarrassment, and then circumstances required it to be dug up and buried again somewhere else. It was a troublesome corpse, perpetually shifting ground. It was photographed demeaningly, feet first, looming to the lens, in socks that were tipped with red at the toes—not blood, merely Harry's vulgar taste in footwear. Suspicion fell upon many amiable and amusing people, Harry's widow for one, who was offhand

Something inconvenient in the woods—Shirley MacLaine, John Forsythe, Mildred Natwick, Edmund Gwenn in THE TROUBLE WITH HARRY

about the whole matter and obviously glad to be rid of him: the role was a distinguished and subtle beginning to the prosperous film career of Shirley MacLaine. Then there was a bumbling and slightly worried Edmund Gwenn, who had been out shooting rabbits and was afraid that one of his shots might have eliminated Harry; and his middle-aged partner in guilt and autumnal romance, Mildred Natwick at her best, who had certainly given Harry a blow on the head with her shoe because he assaulted her, although she had never intended to kill him but couldn't be sure that she hadn't. The death, whether a result of murder or of accident or some vagary of fact, was treated with an irritated contempt. Henry Hull as an absent-minded doctor, walking through the woods and reading a book at the same time, stumbled over the body without bothering to look down and see what it was that had momentarily impeded his constitutional. And around them all, bland as butter, the golden sunlight of Vermont in the fall brought its poetry to the russet leaves and cast its cheering glow through windows of pleasant houses; the ambiance was benign. Alternations between location shots of seasonal grace and studio mock-ups of the area for closer views of the numerous burials were not matched to perfection, by any means; but this didn't matter because the unrealism was so quaint in its therapeutic contrast to the customary tensions of thrillers, and even of comedy thrillers. *The Trouble with Harry* remains unique: Hitchcock's irreverent sense of humour was never so relaxed in any of his other films.

It was sharp again, however, in the famous *North by Northwest* (1959): a mistaken identity spy-lark, played to the hilt for comedy, and furnished with outstandingly sophisticated repartee by Ernest Lehman, to which Cary Grant as the hapless pawn and Eva Marie

Cary Grant, Eva Marie Saint, Thomas Jefferson,
Teddy Roosevelt and Abraham Lincoln in NORTH
BY NORTHWEST

Saint as a blonde enigma did lively justice. As they became acquainted aboard a train to Chicago, Grant (as Roger O. Thornhill) lit a cigarette for her, taking the match from his personal match-fold, which bore his initials: "They're my trademark—ROT." "What does the O stand for?" she asked; and he replied, "Nothing." It was Hitchcock's reminder that tongues should remain in cheeks amid the suspenseful situations. These were plentiful, and several of them have classic quality, losing no excitement when one sees them again and again. A villain pours the greater part of a bottle of bourbon down Grant's throat, and bundles him into an unfamiliar car, leaving him alone in it, to drive very drunkenly along a cliff road high above the sea; luckily he doesn't go over—he crashes into a police car instead. Some little time later, in the public lounge of the United Nations building, we have a jaunty throwback to a Hitchcock kick from *The 39 Steps* (1935): in the middle of a conversation, a UN delegate gives a sudden gasp and collapses into the unlucky arms of Grant, who perceives a knife embedded in the man's back, while press photographers snap the incriminating image; thereafter, Roger O. Thornhill is "wanted for murder on every front page in America." His O for "nothing" has a triple meaning: (a) the movie is intentional nonsense, although its title could suggest that its levity is "but mad north-north-west" and the comedy is by no means devoid of social comment (Robin Wood has examined its serious implications in his book *Hitchcock's Films*); (b) there is no such person as the secret agent "George Kaplan" for whom Thornhill has been mistaken by the henchmen of an enemy agent—"Kaplan" is a myth invented by the U.S. Intelligence to mislead the villains; (c) Thornhill-Kaplan is a human without identity, deprived of the slick security of his real self—the Madison Avenue advertising executive, affluent, neat, and slightly vulgar with his initialled status-symbol match-fold. For him there is sex in a sleeping berth, but terror everywhere else. A mysterious assignation at Prairie Stop, yellow-filtered suspense in sunlight, leaves him stranded and vulnerable in a vast landscape where he is attacked by a "crop-dusting" 'plane. Again, at a snobbish auction where he can see that the villains have him cornered, he disrupts the assembly by making a bid of thirteen dollars for a "Louis Quinze carved and gilded *lit de repos*" and shouting wildly "That's more than it's worth"—until the auctioneer and the well-heeled bidders take him for a lunatic and call the police to carry him away, which was exactly what he wanted. An amalgam of quick-wittedness and improbable fortune, mostly the latter, keeps him alive in his nothingness: his "death" by gunshot in a cafeteria is not a real death because the blonde enigma was firing a blank cartridge. The ultimate muddlesome escape in a way-out chase sequence around the giant stone faces of U.S. presidents, carved upon the heights of Mount Rushmore, remains blissfully absurd over the years.

9. The Mavericks

ONE COULD SAY, broadly, that the decade had been divided between lowbrow bonanzas on big screens and socially orientated movies for intellectuals. The division hardly does justice to the variety of work that existed within each of those categories. In fact, there were no categories of consequence; and this in itself was a sign that Hollywood had advanced, perforce, beyond the pigeon-holing of previous decades. Obviously there were fashions, dictated by commerce. There were also the occasional movies which did not conform to fashion: the mavericks that strayed from the herd. Some of these were made by fairly conformist directors. Vincente Minelli, for example, had made *An American in Paris* (1951) and *Gigi* (1957), two popular big-scale musicals, and between them he had directed a variety of other subjects in his efficient way, often with great style but usually with studio-bound submission to the box-office. And yet, in 1956, Minnelli was somehow able to film *Lust for Life*: a maverick movie, indeed; a remarkable advance upon the cloying film-biographies of famous people. He drew from Kirk Douglas a formidable performance as Vincent van Gogh, and from Anthony Quinn a robust impression of Gauguin, in a film to savage the spirit and enrich the eye. The painter's solitary art and personal torment were marvellously well expressed. Full dramatic advantage was taken, needless to say, of the famous crisis when Van Gogh slashed off his ear with a razor, but this was germane to the theme; the greater value lay in a viably romanticised exploration of the artist at work. Minnelli outpaced the inherent drama of the story with visuals that caught the spirit of Van Gogh's painting, in settings which often reproduced the famous canvasses: the yellow chair stood upon the red-tiled floor of the room at Arles, the *Terrasse de Café* glowed in gaslight beneath a rich dark sky. Above all, the sun and the air of Provence were palpable. The craggy face of Douglas, beneath the broad-brimmed straw hat, caught the very essence of the artist in decline.

Likewise the veteran John Ford, with *Wagonmaster* (1950) to begin the decade and *The Horse Soldiers* (1959) to indicate that his traditional form was pretty substantial in changing times, had gone off at a very unlikely tangent in 1953, regardless of the big-screen frenzy, and made a self-indulgent throwback in black-and-white on a screen of normal shape, *The Sun Shines Bright*. It was defiantly old-fashioned, based on some of the Judge Priest stories of Irvin S. Cobb and set in Kentucky around the turn of the century. Back in the Thirties, Ford had made a movie called *Judge Priest* with Will Rogers in the role that was played now by Charles Winninger: the warm-hearted right-minded man of law, taking the side of a Negro indicted for rape, recognising the heart of gold beneath the paint of a prostitute, and bringing small-town bigots to heel. It was the quintessence of corn, but it smacked of truth at the same time because its basic values were sound, and it was a film made from the heart.

Old-fashioned elements were employed in a sophisticated manner for another of the maverick movies, *The Night of the Hunter* (1955), the first and only film directed by Charles Laughton. Robert Mitchum gave his finest performance as the insane preacher, lusting for money and also for vengeance against the sinful. The primitive situations were given metaphorical power by Laughton's defiant use of throwback styles, including the "iris-out," reminiscent of Griffith, and the strong black-and-white contrasts of light and shadow, a heritage of expression-ist cinema. The floating hair of Shelley Winters, dead at the bottom of a river, and the lyrical yet terrorised flight of two children across a horizon viewed patiently by the preacher, were but two examples of Laughton's relish for the image. And his major set piece, which haunts the memory, had Lillian Gish joining Mitchum in ironic religious duet ("Leaning—leaning—leaning on the everlasting arms"): she indoors with a shotgun at dead of night, wakefully protecting the children in her charge, while he sat in the open across the way, biding his time.

It was sad that Laughton should have waited so long to show us that he could command the screen as a director, more powerfully than he had done at the peak of his career as an actor. For an actor to direct was regarded in Hollywood as a maverick activity in any case, although some actors persevered. Orson Welles, a maverick by nature, directed another Hollywood movie after cosmopolitan wanderings. His *Touch of Evil* (1958) had a typical Wellesian look: chiaroscuro, near to nightmare. On the frontier between the U.S.A. and Mexico, the explosion of a time bomb in a car was the payoff of the first single take, a long one with an amazingly mobile camera that led the eye at the director's command. Watching it, one remembered how Welles, more than Hitchcock, had mastered the intricacies of the long take, in opposition to the familiarity of frequent cuts within a given set-up. Part of the trick is to know just when and for how long to do it, and this was something Welles had judged to perfection before, notably in *The Magnificent Ambersons* (1942) and *The Stranger* (1946). By 1958, too late, Hollywood was ready for Welles—or almost ready. His well-known conflicts with the Hollywood establishment at the start of his cinema career, nearly two decades before, had sent him pell-mell into broader and fresher areas of the world, to struggle and to inspire. *Touch of Evil* can be seen as a bridge from the past to the future in Hollywood's changing pattern. It was individual: unquestionably a *film d'auteur*. It had great style, flamboyant but thrilling. It was a thriller, with a plot which could have served any commonplace production, but Welles lifted it into a richer and more complex sphere and, surrounded by a diversity of characters, dominated the screen himself as a gross detective, steeped in corruption, faking evidence against a killer and turning out, just by chance, to have picked the right culprit: a study in the abuse of power.

Welles maintained the ability to direct a movie superbly while at the same time playing the leading role himself. It is an uncommon gift. In the Fifties, a number of Hollywood actors tried their hands at direction. Burt Lancaster was one: *The Kentuckian* (1955), an unremarkable movie, was his only attempt. He starred as well, and he also produced it, which in his own estimation was "taking on a lot. I knew that when I started. The problem that I had in a town like Hollywood, being known as an actor, was that no one would give me a job as a director. Fortunately, having my own company, I was able to direct a picture on my own. But I must say I think it is a mistake to try to act *and* direct, because directing is a twenty-four-hour-a-day job, and if you are a

197

sincere actor you spend an enormous amount of time on your acting role and it's very difficult to split yourself between the two. Something must suffer. If and when I direct another film, I will not act in it." This opinion was prevalent among those actors who directed movies. Welles remained the giant exception. Laughton had been wise enough not to try both tasks at once; and the same applied to Karl Malden (*Time Limit,* 1957), Dick Powell (*Split Second,* 1952; *The Conqueror,* 1955; *The Enemy Below,* 1957; *The Hunters,* 1958), and James Cagney (*Short Cut to Hell,* 1956: a heavy-weather remake of Frank Tuttle's 1942 thriller *This Gun for Hire,* based on Graham Greene's novel *A Gun for Sale*).

It was a time when studios were torn between the known recipes for security, some as popular as ever, some losing favour with the public, and the slightly desperate expediency to try anything for a change. Therefore mavericks could be given their heads. New men of possible value could take a chance with Hollywood money. Some would survive, although it wasn't easy for either the financiers or the public to be sure how embryonic talents would develop. Who could have supposed, looking at *Teenage Caveman* in 1958, that its young director, Roger Corman, would become a cult idol for a later generation?

The safer bets were placed on the established men, who had weathered previous decades and could usually be relied upon to turn their hands to anything within reason and come up with a work of polish and acceptable style. Typical of this breed was William Wyler, equally at home with the sprawling range of *The Big Country* (1958), which he co-produced with Gregory Peck (who was one of its stars), and with the romantic comedy of *Roman Holiday* (1953). In fact, *Roman Holiday* quietly epitomised the resilience of Wyler. Always a man to draw the best from his players, he launched Audrey Hepburn upon her Hollywood career in this oddly touching hangover from the vogue of the Forties: just on the right side of sentimentality and implausibility, it told of a princess who cut loose from her royal duties and indulged, mildly, in a transient rapport with an exceptionally couth reporter (Gregory Peck). Wyler imparted both humour and a delicate charm, slightly out of fashion but much appreciated by contrast to realistic essays or coarser comedies on the subject of love embattled by convention.

Among the adopted directors, working for Hollywood abroad, the

Englishman David Lean brought a trenchant style to another fleeting romance in *Summertime* (1955: U.K. title, *Summer Madness*), based on the Arthur Laurents play *The Time of the Cuckoo*. Wafting lyrically around Venice, a forlorn American woman encountered a traditionally Latin man and knew unprecedented rapture for a time, departing by train with the image of the city growing ever smaller across the watery horizon: sweet bitterness, astutely conveyed by Katharine Hepburn, mistress of the brimming eye and trembling lip, while Lean's clear vision made sure that the basic intelligence of the material was never swamped in sob-stuff, as it would almost certainly have been a decade earlier.

The romantic love story had even assumed a maverick status for a while during the Fifties. Probably the equivalent of old Hollywood romance, and of numerous B movies of the past, could be left to TV, for which the major studios had begun to make special product in any case. The venerable policy, "if you can't lick 'em, join 'em," was pursued concurrently with the drive to make bigger and more expensive efforts to bring the public back to the cinemas. It was, indeed, a paradoxical decade. In the middle of it, Disneyland was built on Californian soil, an amusement park compounded of movie dreams and money, like a symbol of the childish beam in Hollywood's tired old eye. Before long, that eye would widen in amazement as harbingers of a different kind of cinema, the *nouvelle vague* of France, acknowledged their debt and affection for Hollywood movies. Here were mavericks, speaking words of praise for veterans. And the minorities who attended U.S. art houses were growing all the time: a maverick public. The internationalism that Hollywood had boasted about as it ventured abroad on location, imposing its own ways wherever it went, had become a more meaningful thing. The Hollywood cinema was not the only kind of cinema. This was a shock. It took some time to assimilate. But somehow Hollywood managed, not without difficulty, to maintain itself. The sunset wasn't final, but the breeze at dawn was sharp. Constitutions were shaken a bit. Resilience was needed. Because, not for the first time, change was in the air.

Kirk Douglas in LUST FOR LIFE

Index

(Major references to films appear in bold type)